DOVER SOLO

Swimming the English Channel

DOVER SOLO

Swimming

the English Channel

MARCIA CLEVELAND

DEDICATION

To Mark who remains with
me every stroke of the way.

CONTENTS

CAST OF CHARAC

MARK GREEN: My husband. He was my designated "trainer" and accompanied me on all my major swims leading up to and including the English Channel.

TERRY TYNER: Our good friend and my designated "crew" member during my Channel swim.

ROBERT MAKATURA: My first training partner. He swam the Channel in August 1996.

MARCY MACDONALD: Another one of my training partners. She first swam the Channel in June 1994. As of July 2007, she has nine crossings to her name, and counting. She was the first American woman to complete a 2-way in July 2001.

BECKY FENSON: Another training partner. She swam the Channel in August 1996.

NORA TOLEDANO CADENA: A Mexican swimmer whom I met in Dover just before my swim. She gave me lots of last minute advice and reassurance. She has swum the Channel six times, to date, including a Two Way Swim in August 1994, for which I was part of her crew. Her 2003 book, *A cada Brazada: El Azul Interminable*, recounts her experiences in the Channel.

´ERS

AUDREY AND BILL HAMBLIN: Owners of Victoria Guest House, my "Channel Home" in Dover.

MIKE ORAM: Boat Pilot of *Aegean Blue*. He is now the Honorary Secretary of the Channel Swimming & Piloting Federation.

LANCE ORAM: First mate on *Aegean Blue* during my swim, and Mike's son.

JOSH ALLEN: My Boat Pilot during my three week training camp in Maine.

CAROLYN CLEVELAND: My mother. She spent one week with me in Maine and came to England during my swim.

ROBERT CLEVELAND: My father. He spent one week with me in Maine.

GAIL HAMEL: One of my two sisters. She and her husband, Dave, spent one week with me in Maine, along with their two sons, Mark and Brian who were respectively two years old and 2 1/2 months; they're teenagers now.

PREFACE

The purpose of this book is twofold:
To help future Channel swimmers with their attempts
and to create a memoir of the process
leading up to my swim in 1994.

There is no sure-fire, guaranteed way to swim the English
Channel.
All swimmers will make their attempts in different ways.
This narrative represents what worked for me.

INTRODUCTION

THE ENGLISH CHANNEL IS THE BODY OF water separating the North Sea from the Atlantic Ocean and the British Isles from the European continent. At its narrowest point, the Channel measures 23.69 land miles from Dover, England, to Cap Gris Nez, France. This section is known as "The Strait of Dover." The average water temperature during the summer months is about 60°F. This area either makes you famous or makes you frustrated.

In 1875, Captain Matthew Webb became the first person to swim the English Channel. He did it in 21 hours 45 minutes, swimming breaststroke the whole way, sipping beef tea and warm brandy occasionally passed to him from his escort boat. He used no artificial assistance whatsoever. All he wore was a bathing suit, a bathing cap, goggles, and grease.

The first woman to swim the English Channel was Gertrude Ederle in 1926. Her time of 14 hours 39 minutes set an overall record for men and women at that time. In

July 1978, Penny Dean, an American woman, swam the Channel in a remarkable 7 hours, 40 minutes, which stood as the overall record for 16 years, shattering the previous record of 8 hours, 45 minutes, set by Nasser El Shazley of Egypt in 1977. On September 27, 1994, Chad Hundeby, a 23-year-old American man, rocketed across the Channel in 7 hours, 17 minutes, establishing a new mark. This mark was surpassed by Christof Wandratsch of Germany who established the new standard at 7 hours, 3 minutes, 52 seconds in August 2005. A year later, in August 2006, Yvetta Hlavacova from the Czech Republic broke Penny Dean's 28-year old women's mark with a swim of 7 hours, 25 minutes. On August 24, 2007, Petar Stoychev from Bulgaria became the first person to swim the English Channel in under 7 hours, with a new global standard of 6 hours, 57 minutes, 50 seconds.

"Despite the march of time and progress, the basic essentials of Channel swimming remain precisely the same. Whatever the era, a Channel swim is, and always will be, a battle of one small swimmer against the sometimes savage vastness of the open sea," as quoted from the 1994 edition of the *Channel Swimming Association Handbook*.

Since 1875, more people have been in outer space than have swum the English Channel. Over 7000 swimmers have attempted to emulate Captain Webb's feat; through November 2007, only 1364 of these attempts have been successful. Hence, the odds of success are now about 1 in 6.

The average time for a crossing is slightly less than 13 hours.

In recent years the success rate has improved due mainly to more experienced boat pilots, technological advancements, and training improvements. Swimmers today have the benefit of history from which to learn. When I first wrote *Dover Solo*, between 1875 and the end of 1994, there had been 189 successful solo swims from France to England and 495 successful solos from England to France. These are considered "One Way" swims. Also during this time span, there had been 20 successful Two Way swims (England to France and back to England or vice versa) and three successful Three Way swims (three consecutive laps across the Channel), for a total of 684 solos crossings and 49 multiples. For regular updates on these numbers, please visit www.channelswimming.net and www.Channel-Swims.info

On July 29, 1994, I made the 469th successful solo crossing, from England to France, becoming the 445th person in history to swim the English Channel.

ONE

About Me

IT SEEMS SOME PEOPLE ARE BORN WITH the desire to swim the English Channel; I wasn't one of them. I have been a swimmer nearly my entire life. It is one of those things I can always remember doing. But using my swimming as a way of crossing the English Channel was not one of my life-long, romantic visions. I did it because I thought I could.

It became a focus for three years of my life. During this time, I prepared myself in many different ways for one of the greatest challenges in this world, with no assurances or guarantees that my carefully laid plans would actually work.

I am the third daughter born to my parents, Carolyn and Bob, and I was quickly followed by a brother. Our family started out in Pennsylvania and eventually settled in Connecticut.

By the time I was a year-and-a-half old, Mom and

Dad had gotten tired of retrieving me fully clothed from the bottom of swimming pools so they taught me how to swim.

I graduated quickly from the splash phase in the baby pool and went on to my competitive career. During my third summer, I was entered in a race consisting of one width of the "big" (adult) pool. It was during this same summer that I started jumping off the diving board and swimming to the side, unassisted.

I liked being in the water; the cool, fluid feeling surrounded me and kept me buoyant. During the winters my mother would take me to the local indoor pool and we did laps together. It never occurred to me that I was the youngest in the pool by a few decades. I was simply where I wanted to be.

I swam on summer teams and joined a year-round program when I was eight: Sharks Swim Team. I was on the varsity swim team at Greenwich High School, achieving All-American status. While at Yale University, I swam on the varsity team for four years. Despite all this swimming, I always felt I could have been a better swimmer. I wished I could do something more with my swimming. I believed there was something out there that would make me feel I had really accomplished something. I wanted to prove it to myself.

It was at Sharks that I first started to understand the results of consistent effort. Under the coaching of Walter Rothenheber and Mark Newcombe, I worked hard to achieve my goals. Being motivated towards something I personally consider achievable gets my engine revving.

After graduating from Yale, I moved to New York City and worked at an advertising agency. It was there that I met my husband, Mark Green. We were married in September 1990.

One of the things I found so attractive about Mark was that although he did not swim much himself (though he did pass his 'Pre-Marital Swim Test'), he supported my swimming from the very start of our relationship. He knew it was something that made me happy and content and he never felt threatened by it. Neither of us knew where my swimming was heading; I just kept on swimming because I liked it.

In New York City, I joined a Masters team and became part of United States Masters Swimming. Founded in 1970, USMS is an organization dedicated to promoting lifetime fitness and health in adults by offering a variety of programs for swimming enthusiasts throughout the United States. In 1994, there were about 30,000 registered USMS swimmers in the country. This number has ballooned to over 43,000 in 2007.

TWO

First Thoughts

I WAS ALWAYS A POOL SWIMMER BECAUSE the mysterious unknowns of open water swimming scared me. The differences between pool swimming and open water swimming are analogous to those of running on a track and running cross country. The sport mechanics are similar but the environments are completely different. During the eight years I lived in New York City, I swam with many people who were seasoned open water swimmers and they gradually drew me to it. Surprisingly, I began to enjoy it.

Over the next few years, as I swam outdoors more and more, I started to feel comfortable in this environment and began to conquer some of my fears. Soon I entered local 1-and 2-mile open water races and found I enjoyed them.

The entire open water scene is different from pool swimming and competition. The races usually begin with a mass start from the water's edge with swimmers charging towards the water. After about a quarter of a mile from this initial charge, the faster and slower swimmers tend to sort out; this is where I often begin to establish a rhythm. Most open water swim races require the finishers to run a short distance out of the water to the finish line. The whole experience is pretty exciting, sometimes very hard, and most often, fun.

My focus in swimming started to shift as I discovered that I loved the freedom and variety of open water swimming. I love the wide open space without boundaries. I love stroking through the water, being enveloped by it, feeling my body rotate with every pull, and leaving a long wake behind. I love being rocked by the swells of the changing tides and inhaling the salt air on every breath. I love glancing down to catch the occasional glimpse of marine life. I love watching the sun rise from the water. I love swimming fast enough to work up a sweat and breathe hard. I love the clean way my skin and hair feel after a swim. In the fall, I love watching the leaves on the trees turn from green to orange, yellow, and red, and the way the water becomes crystal clear. I love sharing these feelings with other people who have experienced similar sensations.

The Start

In August 1991, I swam in my first marathon swim, the Manhattan Island Marathon Swim, around the island of Manhattan, a distance of 28 1/2 miles. This annual race attracts a field of international swimmers of varying ability levels. It starts at The Battery (the southern tip of Manhattan Island), proceeds north up the East and Harlem Rivers, then heads south down the Hudson River, finishing at The Battery. As I was passing the World Trade Center near the end of the race, I suddenly thought, "This race has been a piece of cake. I think I'll try the English Channel."

By the time I finished the race, I knew in what direction I was headed. During the next month, I decided I would make my attempt in 1994 as a 30th birthday present to myself. I told Mark matter-of-factly in September 1991 what my newest long range, big goal was and he replied simply "OK." Because he had so much confidence in me, he knew if I made such a statement, I would, in fact, swim the English Channel.

PUTTING THE PIECES TOGETHER

A few days after I told Mark my future swimming plans, I met with two swimmer friends in New York. One had coached the other to a successful Channel swim in 1989. After watching the finish of my Manhattan swim, one of them told me she had thought at the time, "Marcia should do the Channel." Their helpful guidance and support enabled me to examine my motives for swimming the Channel. The reason I was attempting to swim the English Channel was simply because I thought I could.

I am a firm believer in preparation. Difficult training conditions had to be simulated. After identifying the components and breaking them down into pieces, I set out to deal with each one. For the next three years I did something key to succeeding at anything: I sweated the details.

From what I could gather, some of the components to swimming the English Channel were:

- Being prepared to swim in 55° to 60° Fahrenheit (F) salt water for over 14 hours.
- Acquiring the necessary swimming endurance.
- Researching the swim.
- Swimming in challenging weather conditions (waves and swells, wind and fog).
- Swimming with marine life (jellyfish, seaweed, fish, etc.) and through jetsam and flotsam. (Jetsam is man-made debris, flotsam is organic matter such as seaweed.)
- Swimming at night.
- Swimming across one of the busiest shipping lanes in the world.
- Dealing with the mental stress.
- Dealing with nausea while swimming.
- Selecting a boat pilot.
- Inhaling exhaust fumes from a boat while swimming and not getting sick.
- Practicing being fed while treading water, with the emphasis on simplicity and speed.
- Keeping track of what works (and what doesn't work).
- Testing and practicing with the equipment.
- Practice, practice, practice!

From 1991 to 1993, I kept my goal mainly to myself, sharing it with only a few family members and close friends. During this time I looked at my training and knew I would have to make adjustments. I set up a long-range training schedule and gradually increased my swimming yardage to a level which would give me the endurance base to swim the distance.

I read everything I could find on the Channel: articles, books, newspapers; and I compiled extensive notes. Based on what I read, I thought I could swim the Channel in 10 to 14 hours if I had decent conditions. The people who were successful were heroic in my eyes, and I learned a lot from their methods. However, it was the ones who failed who intrigued me and made me want to know why they had failed. What had they missed in their preparations that resulted in an unsuccessful swim? Sometimes the weather turns bad and ends a swim, which is unfortunate. Some gave up within 2 miles of the coast they were swimming towards. Some gave up within 2 miles of the coast they were swimming from. WHY? There are thousands of reasons why swims are aborted and I wanted to make sure that I dealt with each and every one of them.

During these years I learned to accept what I had to do in order to swim the Channel. I was ready for this challenge that would affect most aspects of my life.

The most important component was acclimating to cold water. can not emphasize this enough and it is one of the main keys to any successful swim. Before my Channel swim, I decided I needed to be ready to endure 14 or more hours in 58°F water, assisted only by feedings every half-hour. This was a scary thought.

When I first learned that the water temperature in the Channel was about 60°F, I was bug-eyed scared and thought, "How am I going to get around this?" Basically, I was not, nor are you.

Sometimes things in life are perfectly straight forward. The only way to learn to swim in cold water is to consistently swim in cold water. Over time, the human body acclimates to colder temperatures so it gets a little easier to enter and stay in cold water, but it never gets easy. It was only later that I discovered that, regardless of experience, 'everybody shakes' when they've been in cold water for long enough. During that first Fall in 1992 it was incredibly tough for me. There is simply no magic pill you can take to make acclimation any easier. Believe me—I would have found it!

THE KEY TO ACCLIMATION

Safety is the most important aspect of open water swimming. Having a partner or an escort boat is critical. In cold water swimming, the safety factor is even more important because of the possibility of hypothermia.

In September 1992 I started to swim every weekend in the Atlantic Ocean at Rockaway, Queens. The first time I swam alone, and it was awful. I don't like to swim alone because of the scary monsters circulating through my imagination. When I first swam at Rockaway, I swam parallel to the beach, never more than 25 yards off shore. The waves were breaking in this shallow water but I was too frightened to go out further where the water was calmer and deeper. It was a good self-taught lesson on how to swim in swells and to tolerate chop.

The Rockaway Beaches have pilings jutting out from the shore lines to help control beach erosion. Short wood stumps are placed in a line starting around the high tide mark and extending out into the water about 30 yards. Pilings give the sand a physical structure to hit against instead of being washed out to sea. I didn't know that the pilings extended underwater so I gave myself quite a scare early on when unknowingly I stood on one and slipped, cutting my legs in the process and screaming because, in my mind, I knew Jaws had me. After this incident, I sprinted past the pilings.

Amazingly, the longer I was immersed that day, the more comfortable I became; it actually was quite pleasant to be in the ocean. I even saw the Concorde take off. The water quality was a little dubious though. It was so brown and murky I could not see my hand unless it was practically in front of my face. To top it off, I found out afterwards that this brown, murky water was a direct result of a broken sewage pipe nearby. Yuck. I lasted half an hour in 68°F sewage water, not exactly an extraordinary feat of bravery or endurance.

My First Training Partner

I had a problem. I had to find a swimming partner since it would have taken inordinate psychological measures for me to swim alone. Beyond the fact that it wasn't safe and I did not feel comfortable by myself, I was downright scared.

That week, Mark and I were at a friend's apartment and I secretly confessed to her that I wanted to swim the Channel. She told me she had a friend who was also thinking along those same lines. If I agreed, she would mention it to him. My phone at work rang at 9 a.m. the next day—this was my introduction to Robert Makatura. We set up a time to swim that weekend at Rockaway.

Robert and I had known each other casually through swimming in New York. In the 1991 Manhattan Island Marathon Swim, he finished 4th overall and I was 5th. We have become extremely good friends and have shared some amazing experiences through the years. By swimming

Robert & Me at Greenwich Point, Fall 1992.

together, our shared knowledge of open water swimming has been enormously enhanced and keeps growing.

The next weekend, in 64°F water, Robert and I swam for more than an hour in five to eight foot swells. It felt so comforting to have someone alongside, especially since Robert and I had similar goals and abilities.

We swam together every weekend for the next six weeks in many different types of conditions. We challenged ourselves to swim for progressively longer times in water that was gradually cooling off at a rate of about 2°F a week. Sure, our skin felt as though it was burning initially, but after about five minutes, both of us were OK. (THIS IS NORMAL.) There would be the inevitable dreaded cold patches and we got through them fast even though there would always be more. The changing autumn colors were beautiful and made fall swimming all that more pleasurable. I always felt at ease swimming with Robert.

Before each swim, we would set intermediate and ultimate goals for ourselves such as, "Let's try to swim for an hour in this 55°F water but if we make it for an hour and a half or, ultimately, two hours, that would be great."

Without fail, the hardest part, always, was getting started. During that fall, Robert and I met every one of our ultimate goals and helped to demystify cold water training for ourselves. By doing it, we were learning just how hard it would be to swim the Channel. During our last swim on November 7, 1992, the air temperature was 38°F and the skies were overcast. We swam for an hour in 51°F water.

Robert and I learned a lot that fall, mostly through trial and error. Sometimes we would swim in deep swells 300 yards off shore at Rockaway. In these deep waters, clouds of yellow and green phosphorescent specks would float up to us as we solidly stroked parallel to the shore, the bottom nowhere in sight. The greenish water simply descended into spooky darkness but Robert's presence made me feel safe and helped me develop courage. Being so far from the beach made me nervous, and I also realized how tenuous all of this was, how much on the edge it was. It made me realize we were unique and special in doing this; we weren't beginners anymore.

Mark came to Rockaway once. From his place on the beach, he twice saw small power boats pass between the shoreline and where Robert and I were swimming; both of us were completely oblivious to these boats. This made Mark understandably nervous since he would be virtually helpless to assist us if anything happened. We should have been smarter about where we swam.

During all these ocean swims, I did not fully realize how much strength and endurance I was gaining. Just dealing with the swells and having to sight by looking forward forced me to develop lots of upper body strength.

Because we would swim so far off shore, swimming into the beach would often take a few minutes. I have always loved to body surf but these long swims tired me out and made body surfing a chore. Instead of battling the waves, I just wanted to be on terra firma again. Nevertheless, it was all part of the "process."

We met Joy Rosenberg, another open water swimmer, on the beach at Rockaway. She lived two blocks from the beach and was kind enough to let us use the outdoor shower at her house after our swims. Joy swims near the shore, in between two sets of pilings, an area she calls her "Bay." She is an extremely enthusiastic young-looking woman in her mid-50s, a real testament to the effects of lifetime exercise. Her mind is sharp, her body well-toned and her face just naturally glows. She usually swims outdoors until Thanksgiving simply because she loves it. When we met her 26-year-old son, he commented, "So you're crazy like my mom!"

Bracing ourselves at the start of a swim, Robert and I step into 55 water, Fall 1992.

Do it Now! No Turning Back!

After dealing with rough ocean conditions at Rockaway, in mid-October, Robert and I started swimming at Greenwich Point (also known as Tod's Point) in Connecticut on Long Island Sound. The protected conditions on the Sound made the water a little calmer. We were interested in acclimating ourselves as opposed to beating ourselves up in the ocean. Every weekend, as the water continued to get a few degrees cooler, we did some strong mental gymnastics to get in. Consistency was important at this point. Going from 58°F to 55°F water in one week wasn't as much of a shock as plunging right into 55°F water without any previous exposure, and something I would not advise.

Robert and I would get ready in the car (suits, caps and goggles on, Vaseline applied) and walk quickly across the beach to the water. It would have been so easy to stop and trot back to the warmth of the car. There wasn't anyone standing around making either of us do this; it was something from within, the desire and the drive to succeed, knowing this was one of the stepping stones in the process. To give in would have meant having to get through this some other time, or even giving up the entire project. An unspoken agreement developed between us: we would do it now; neither of us ever suggested getting back in the car.

There was no easy, leisurely warm-up period to these swims. We waded into waist-level water in about a minute and then swam fast right from the start. There were times I thought my feet would break off because they were so cold. Churning my arms through the water at 80 strokes per minute, counting 1-2-3 arm strokes, breathe, 1-2 arm strokes, breathe, 1-2-3, breathe, 1-2, breathe, and on and on. My limbs and face felt as if they were on fire and my skin burned for the first few minutes, then seemingly miraculously, I would be OK.

We did laps parallel to the shore, each about 800–1000 yards in length. In between these laps, we rested and stretched by treading water for about a minute, conferring about whatever we needed to, like course and direction, pace, any thoughts we were having, as bizarre as they might be. The time varied slightly in one direction, depending on which way the tide and currents were running. Of course, if there was a reason to stop in the middle of a lap that was OK, but we got to the point where we didn't need to.

As the water became colder each weekend, Robert and I would take fewer breaks during our swims to talk. My hands were constantly moving forward, searching for any warmer water. I found that after a while, my fingers tended to curl up and conk out, to the point where I felt as if I was pulling my fist through the water, instead of my flat, extended hand which was so much more efficient. When the water was in the very low 50s, I thought almost exclusively about getting warm in the immediate future.

During these swims, Robert and I monitored one another to make sure each of us was still all right. We would swim next to each other, look into each other's eyes every five breaths or so and silently assure one another, "Yes, you're OK."

Freezing . . . and Defrosting!

We also asked each other simple questions to test mental lucidity and current verbal skills. When we first began to swim together, we agreed to end a swim if either of us decided we had had "enough," or exhibited severe hypothermia.

Hypothermia is the body's inability to keep itself warm and a condition that only worsens until the source (such as cold water) is curtailed and the affected person can warm up. Uncontrollable shivering and slurred speech are signs of mild to moderate hypothermia. Loss of mental acuity, ataxia, and loss of consciousness show up in the advanced phase.

By swimming together, Robert and I learned each other's limits. These experiences made me a believer in having either a swimming partner or an escort boat with an observer during cold water swims.

It was at Greenwich Point that I experienced my first real bouts with mild hypothermia. As it progressed, my speech would slur, sounding as if I were talking with marbles in my mouth. When I got out of the water, my teeth chattered and I shook uncontrollably, sometimes for hours. This is a NORMAL survival instinct. Hypothermia affects you at the neuromuscular level and it takes time for the body to recover. Fortunately, I always remained lucid and never became ataxic. To keep the cold water from penetrating my ears, I used Murine ear drops because they leave a thick coating. Ear plugs are also effective. Both during and after these swims, my fingers and hands would cramp so badly (self-labeled "Channel Cramp") that they would be useless for quite a while. It would take me 20 minutes in a 116°F shower to straighten them out. Trying to pull my bathing cap down over my ears mid-swim or to use car keys immediately afterwards were lost causes. More than once we had to ask a perplexed observer to open the car door as we stood there on a late fall afternoon dripping wet and shaking uncontrollably.

At the end of our swims, Robert and I would run from the water to the car, somehow get the doors open (often with help), grab towels and barely dry off, then climb inside the car and blast the heat as we attempted to dry our shaking limbs and put on layers of clothing over our suits. Wearing a ski hat helped curb heat loss for me. When some of our shaking subsided, one of us would drive the car to my mom's house where hot showers awaited. Even with the heat in the car, the layers of warm clothing, and the long, hot shower, it would usually take me a few hours to stop shivering. Over time, I have learned that everyone, regardless of cold water experience, shakes.

I understood early on, when I was in there freezing my butt off, that if I stayed in water that cold too long, I could die of exposure. Hypothermia strikes quickly and needs to be recognized and treated rapidly.

When the water started to get colder (55°F and below) that fall, I grasped at any trick to stay warm, thinking of hot things which would help keep me mentally warmed and physically fooled. Hot showers, mittens and flannel pajamas were favorite distractions. I sang endless verses of *My Favorite Things* to myself. I would also think about where I was feeling the cold and what body parts were changing temperatures (cold to warm/hot or vice versa.) At one point, without any programming, I started to sing Cole Porter's song, *Too Darn Hot*, which especially helped distract me from the cold. One of my friends joked about piloting an ice breaker boat next to me when I swam. Visualizing this cracked me up!

Early in October, I realized that if I didn't shave my legs, I would have one more edge against the cold. Anything that worked.

For some reason, when I was at my most desperately cold, I learned to think of Mark. I imagined his arms wrapped tightly around me. He would often hold onto me like this after my exhausting cold water swims, and in his furnace-like way, slowly help me reverse the drastic heat-escape going on within. I thought of this when I was swimming and it made me feel like I was covered with a warm blanket. Mark and I both found it incredibly ironic that I could swim in water that just cracked 50°F but shiver on land for hours afterwards despite the hot showers, layers of warm clothing, and Mark's long, warm hugs. The cold water just sapped all my heat.

Mark often came with us to Greenwich Point and stood on the shore wearing his ski hat and jacket as Robert and I swam back and forth along the beach in the late afternoon light of those fall days. What kept us in there was the drive and desire to achieve our goal. I remember the sun setting on Halloween night as we finished that day's 20 hour swim in 55°F water. I had spent these glorious hours watching the beautiful red, orange, and gold fall colors on the trees change with the waning light of the overcast day. It was a beautiful scene from the unique perspective of the water.

Body Changes

A transformation was occurring. During 1992, I shook badly from hypothermia but following a similar routine in the fall of 1993, I barely shook at all. The Channel Cramp in my hands was much less severe in 1993. I had learned that I lost the most heat from my head, armpits, and groin so it was normal for these places to feel the coldest. Before getting in the water, I would usually cover these areas with a thin layer of Vaseline.

In May 1994, I swam in 48°F water at Greenwich Point. This was the most painful entry to any swim I had ever had so far and I thought my ankles were literally going to break off. Of course, in the car on the way to the swim, I lectured my two swimming partners/victims about how "I don't want to hear any complaining about cold water today. It'll hurt just a little bit, then it will be OK."

It was a bright sunny day so the beach was filled with lots of pre-season sunbathers. Some of them watched in amazement as we headed into the water. I even heard one guy claim, "Oh, they're probably wearing grease (we weren't) and will only be in for a minute."

A little while later, standing up to my calves in the coldest water of my life, I really wanted to tell my swimming mates, "Sorry but I just can't do this today. It's just too cold for me."

Somehow I kept silent and kept walking further into the water. I lunged forward and found myself swimming as fast as possible. In a few minutes, amazing things started to happen. I felt a swirling rush of hot blood in my abdomen, obviously sent there by my stressed circulatory system to keep my vital organs warm, and my hands and feet did not feel excruciatingly cold. I even warmed up as I swam. It was as if my internal organs knew what to expect, saying "OK, she's up to her old stuff again but we'll be OK." It had taken two years of extensive cold water training but my body had learned to react. **This is the key to acclimation.**

BUILDING ENDURANCE

My goal was to swim the English Channel. In order to do this, I took a good look at my weekly swimming yardage which I have tracked since I was a teenager. (American swimmers usually keep track of the distance they swim in terms of "yardage." One mile equals 1,760 yards.)

In February 1993, I was swimming less than 20,000 yards a week. If I wanted to swim the Channel, the answer was simple: I had to increase this yardage dramatically in order to have the necessary endurance. After listening to how a few other Channel swimmers had trained, ranging from 25,000 to 50,000 yards a week, I decided to work my way up to 30,000 to 35,000 yards a week by March 1993, then step up my training gradually to 45,000 yards per week by January/February 1994. I picked this specific distance because the English Channel is 23.69 land miles across at its narrowest point (20 nautical miles); 45,000 yards equals 25.5 miles. Swimming the equivalent of the Channel every week for several months would be good practice. To get in this yardage, I swam with a team five times a week and on my own or with a small group four other times a week.

My 1993 open water race season ran from June through September, beginning with the 4.4 mile Chesapeake Bay Swim in Maryland. Results from this swim would help me determine how my training was going. I finished in 1 hour, 51 minutes and felt strong the whole way. The increase in yardage during the past few months was beginning to show some effects; I had set myself up for an excellent summer. Although I did very well in all my races that summer, my prevailing thought during every race was, "I can hardly wait until next summer when it's me and the Channel."

THREE

The Start of the Process

ENGLISH CHANNEL SWIMMERS WHO WISH to have their swim officially recognized must register with either the Channel Swimming & Piloting Federation or the Channel Swimming Association, fill out an application, reserve a pilot boat, and get themselves to the southeastern coast of England.

These two organized bodies validate all attempts to swim across the English Channel. They exist in order to:

1. Investigate and authenticate the claims of persons who have swum the Channel.
2. To assist with information and advise those intending to make attempts.
3. To further the interest in Channel swimming.

More recently, these associations must enforce the rules and regulations of the British and French Coast Guards,

Custom and Immigrations, French and British Courts, and the Dover Harbour Board. They both require swimmers to submit a medical certificate before an application to swim is approved.

The basic swimming rules for a Channel swim, as stated in the Information Packs, are quite straightforward:

- The swim starts on the natural shore, not from a groyne or breakwater.
- The swim finishes on the natural shore, with no sea-water beyond, unless the finish is against steep cliffs, when it is sufficient to touch them with no sea-water beyond.
- The swimmer receives no help and must not be touched by anyone, but may be handed food and drink.
- The swimmer may wear:
  a. only ONE STANDARD swimming cap
  b. only ONE STANDARD swimming costume
  c. goggles, nose-clip, ear plugs, and grease
  d. a light stick at night

The General Rules of Channel Swimming shall apply at all times. These rules stated above were effective in 1994 but all aspiring swimmers and their crew should be thoroughly knowledgeable about the current rules since they are updated periodically.

In addition, Pacers are allowed but must not enter the water without the Boat Pilot's consent. They must not enter the water until the swimmer is at least 2 hours into the swim and must not stay in the water longer than one hour at a time. They must not re-enter the water for at least one hour. No pacers are allowed on relays.

In 1994, the application fee to swim the Channel was £102 Sterling for a solo swim (about US $150 in 1994). This fee included an official observer, all the necessary paperwork, and a one-year membership in the organization with which you are swimming. The Information Packs describes the current rules and conditions. All these materials and more information are available through the Honorary Secretaries; their names and contact information are listed in the Appendix.

In June 1993, I reserved a boat for the first neap tide in August 1994. (This tide fell between July 29 and August 6.) When I made this reservation I felt a nervous sense of commitment and responsibility: "Yes, this is going to happen and you are doing this to yourself."

The full cost of renting a certified boat for a Channel swim was £1000 in 1994, about US $1500. When I reserved his boat, my pilot, Mike Oram, asked for a deposit of £150 to secure my reservation. The £850 balance would be paid in cash before I left the dock on the day of my swim.

The British Government requires that all boat pilots escorting Channel swimmers have licenses and meet qualifications, to preclude "Mr. Acme Fisherman" from being an escort boat for Channel swims. All of the current Channel boat pilots are located in England.

I asked Mike about getting an additional escort boat since I had a lot of enthusiastic family members who were considering coming along. Mike strongly indicated that this was a bad idea. "You'll be in pain and look over at them enjoying themselves and laughing and eating sandwiches and then you'll be mad. Or you'll see them getting seasick."

In addition, using two boats for one swimmer means taking a boat away from another swimmer which Mike would not do. To solve this dilemma, Mark brought along a video camera with two back-up batteries and filmed lots of my swim so everyone who was interested could watch it afterwards. This is still the best solution.

QUALIFYING SWIM

To swim the English Channel, applicants must submit proof in their application of a Qualifying Swim in 60°F water. No formal "Qualifying Swim" exists nor are there any "official" observers for it. (I have developed a standardized letter to send when I ratify a qualifying swim.) Applicants simply find a body of 60°F water and swim in it for six hours or more. In order to protect against lawsuits towards the organizing swim bodies, the person who verifies an applicant's Qualifying Swim is legally responsible for the applicant. The qualifying standard has actually been lowered from ten hours to six because some swimmers attempted their Ten Hour Qualifying Swim in Dover Harbor just a few days before they attempted to swim the Channel and did not allow for nearly enough physical recovery time.

One of the major reasons for this requirement is to test a swimmer's long-term tolerance in cold water and to give aspiring Channel swimmers a taste of what they are getting into. Unfortunately, five people have died trying to swim the English Channel. The first, in the 1950s, was an English father of nine who made the only known solo attempt without a support boat. He towed a small inflatable supply raft behind him, topped with a sign reading "Lone Swimmer." Three weeks after his attempt, his body washed up on a beach in The Netherlands. The next two deaths occurred during the 1980s. In 1999, a woman from Mexico died and in 2001, a man from Switzerland succumbed to 'Channel conditions.'

Marcy—Another Training Partner

Marcy MacDonald and I have known each other since our age group swimming days in Connecticut and have swum in many open water races together. She was also planning to swim the Channel in 1994. In the spring of 1993, we got together a few times to do long swims in Columbia Lake in upstate Connecticut. It was great to compare notes and train with her; during the next year, we spoke every few weeks about our training.

Ten Long Hours in Lake Sunapee

Marcy and I chose to do our ten-hour Qualifying Swim together on Saturday September 25, 1993 in Lake Sunapee, New Hampshire. I thought this would be a fairly leisurely swim and silently speculated that we would goof off a lot, practice some stroke drills, and tread water whenever we felt like it. I was in for a chilling surprise.

Mark and I drove up to New Hampshire on September 24th. From the looks of our car, we may as well have been moving to New Hampshire. Packed were things such as bed linens, pillows and even a space heater. (What was I thinking???)

Marcy reserved cabins on the waterfront. Her family vacationed at this rustic, charming spot when she was younger, so two of her seven siblings came along to help out and reminisce. Her older sister, Joanne, and Joanne's husband, Frankie, brought their four children. Marcy's older brother, Kenny, rented a power boat that proved to be enormously useful during our swim. Everyone was extremely supportive and helpful. I truly doubt I would have made this swim without everyone's assistance that day.

When I woke up at 5 a.m. on Saturday I was nervous. I had not slept well, tossing and turning with anxious energy. I ate a small breakfast, put on my bathing suit and sweats, then walked the short distance to Marcy's cabin to see if she was awake.

She was definitely awake. Marcy was getting her equipment together as Joanne busily cooked breakfast for everyone. Since Joanne was a nurse, she thought it would be a good idea to monitor our temperatures throughout the day and placed a thermometer in each of our mouths. Only after our swims would we find out the results: Marcy's temperature started off at 98.6°F while I registered 97.5°F first thing in the morning.

I returned to our cabin. Mark was now showered and dressed. As is typical on days when he accompanies me on long swims, he did not want to eat anything. I shed my sweats, Mark put on plastic gloves and slathered me with a coat of suntan lotion followed by a coat of grease everywhere, including under my suit. (In hindsight, I do not recommend putting grease under your suit, but I do recommend two coats of suntan lotion and one or two coats of grease just under your suit line, on your legs, back, armpits, and neck.) I had mixed lanolin and Vaseline together (in a 1:2 ratio) the day before in a big plastic container. It is also possible to mix by warming on a stove or heating up in a microwave but regardless of how you do it the outcome is always a gigantic, sticky mess.

Marcy and I came out of our cabins at the same time, looking like white monsters. We headed down to the water's edge where the canoe was docked. It was 6 a.m. We bobbed around in the water for about 15 minutes while Mark and Joanne loaded the canoe with supplies. I was hoping to somehow miraculously acclimate to this freezing cold water in 15 minutes.

On this sparkling clear fall day, the water temperature remained a constant 60°F until 4pm when we finished. Even though I was wearing grease for the first time in my life and had had some exposure to cold water the previous fall, there was never any relief from the cold. I shivered from the start. This Qualifying Swim was also brutal because my weight was very low and I had not yet trained in cold water this fall. The water I had swum in the prior weekend was 72°F! I had to swim hard the whole way just to stay warm.

The only thing I had going for me was conditioning. I would never recommend to anyone such a drastic change in temperature. If it wasn't for Marcy, Mark, and Marcy's fabulous family, I never would have completed this Qualifying Swim at this time. Mark was concerned about my hypothermic condition from the start. Up to this swim, he knew what "good" looked like. That day, he learned what "bad" and "desperado" looked like too.

Marcy's sister, Joanne, and Mark paddled the canoe alongside us. They were magnificent all day. At one point around the sixth hour when Marcy and I were swimming straight into a strong head wind, Joanne's husband, Frankie, relieved her for an hour. Mark stayed in the canoe almost the entire time. Marcy's brother, Kenny, Frankie, and the four children acted as the "ground crew" for the whole day. They endlessly shuttled hot food and drinks in a power boat from land to the canoe. When it was over, they wrapped us in blankets and led us back to our cabins. These people were wonderful and I truly appreciated their generosity.

During long open water swims, swimmers receive nourishment in the form of "feedings." This is the only assistance a swimmer is allowed. These feedings usually consist of some sort of liquid in a cup passed over the side of the boat to the swimmer who momentarily treads water, gulps down the contents, communicates with the crew, and begins swimming again. Ideally, feeding stops should last for no more than 30 to 60 seconds; some very experienced swimmers take less than 10 seconds.

Marcy and I started out with various types of carbohydrate feedings every 20 minutes, a short feeding interval for cold water swims. After 6 1/2 hours, I began feeding at 10 minute intervals which is practically "intravenous." Many of these 10 minute feeds consisted solely of hot water. I didn't need the food—I needed the warmth.

Marcy and I during our Qualifying Swim in Lake Sunapee, NH, September 25, 1993.

Without these frequent feedings, I honestly don't think that I would have been able to finish.

Joanne started taking our temperatures with an oral thermometer every 30 minutes. By the third hour, my temperature had dropped to 95°F (she told me later) and it became hard for me to hold a thermometer in my mouth because my teeth were chattering so much. Joanne soon scrapped the thermometer idea. All day, her poker face yielded no indication—good or bad—of any factual information about us. Within a few hours, my internal temperature gauge was so far out of whack that when we momentarily hit a super-warm spot in a cove, Marcy and I both thought it was about 70°F. We were told after we finished that the area had been only 64°F. As tempting as it was to stay in these sparse warm spots, it made it that much more difficult to go back out into the rest of the freezing cold lake.

In this gorgeous lake surrounded by beautiful fall foliage, I suffered my own private hell. The cold was all-enveloping and my mind played tricks. After about three hours of swimming, I saw an image of Mark's face before me whenever I put my face in the water. Mesmerized, I swam towards it. Although I could never quite catch it, his image kept me moving forward for a while and kept me temporarily distracted from the cold.

During the first few hours, I cheerfully said aloud to myself, "I'm so glad we're doing this," but after about four hours I stopped saying it. Even though Joanne gave us Motrin every two hours to relieve any physical pain we might have, the invasive cold just would not go away. At around 6 1/2 hours, my ability to concentrate became marginal and I became mentally "blah."

I can't emphasize enough how hard it was at this point. Around this time, Mark enthusiastically yelled, "How ya doin'?" to which I quietly responded, "OK." He wanted to know if the power boat should stay close by in case I needed to get out. I told him, "No, not yet." I really didn't think I could endure this for much longer but I wanted to see if I could hang on just a few more minutes. Mark thought I had put my head down to resume swimming when he yelled to Kenny, "Stay with us! She's not doing well!" Even though Mark wished otherwise, I had heard this exchange. Yet even so, I lethargically turned away from the boat and slowly started to swim again.

I visualized what I would look like if I gave up now: a disappointed, beached whale sitting on Kenny's power boat, my white grease and white bathing suit gleaming in the sun. It was here that I realized that I had to earn the right to go to England.

The last four hours of this swim were extremely difficult for me, both physically and mentally. I went through a very down period from the sixth to the eighth hours when this was not fun at all and I thought of giving up. The end was too far away to insure that I would actually make it. Mark and Joanne were wondering how they were going to pull me from the water and leave Marcy in. I started to fantasize about getting my Channel escort boat to hook up a firehouse to spray hot water on me during my Channel swim. (This would be out of the question and in complete violation of Channel rules.)

During this period, my stomach felt very full from the frequent feedings (watery oatmeal, soup, Nutrament, chicken broth, Exceed, and hot water.) But around eight hours, I mentally came back to life and by 8 1/2 hours, I knew I would make it. I was still freezing cold, but I knew I could last until the end since I had come this far and the end was now in sight.

By this time, Marcy and I were almost back to the point from which we had started so we did another loop around the bottom of the cove, the same place where we had first swum in the scant daylight at 6am, killing time, and for me, being scared. The cove looked much more reassuring in the mid-afternoon sunlight as I could now actually see the large dock Marcy had mentioned nine hours earlier. This time I wasn't scared; instead, exasperated feelings of "How much longer can I take this?" filled my head. Marcy didn't want to stop so frequently so she would often swim on ahead while I fed. I was like a small child, staying right along side the boat, taking whatever security it could provide.

Marcy's performance the whole day was impressive. She never complained or seemed bothered by the cold. Her form was solid and her pace was consistent all day. If anyone was prepared for the Channel, it was Marcy. (She now rightfully holds the unofficial title, "American Queen" of the Channel, with 9 laps across the Big Pool.)

Finally, it was over. We had been swimming for 10 hours and now we could stop. After all the "ughs" and hoping for so many long hours for the end to come, Marcy and I had both achieved our goal: to qualify to swim the English Channel. We did it one stroke at a time.

We waded out of the water at the same point we had entered it ten hours before having just swum the entire length and back of Lake Sunapee, about 20 miles round trip. I was tired and cold but at least I could walk. Marcy's family looked just as relieved as we were that it was over as they wrapped us in thermal blankets.

I took a hot shower in our cabin and used Palmolive dishwashing detergent on sponges to get the grease off. My grease-coated bathing suit looked like it had been drenched in Crisco so I threw it out.

Later, Mark and I ate left-over pizza for dinner. This wasn't very nutritious after such a depleting day, but neither of us was very hungry and we were both wiped out. If I had drunk lots of a replenishment fluid and taken Motrin after this swim, I probably would have felt better and recovered more quickly. In any event, I was back to full-time training in about a week.

Channel Gods and the Weather on Sunday

The day after our Qualifying Swim, I woke up at 6 a.m. to the sound of rain pelting our cabin. By mid-morning it turned into a ferocious storm. My shoulders and scapulas ached tremendously; but both Marcy and I were happy, relieved, and lucky to have our Qualifying Swim decisively behind us. The Channel Gods must have been watching over us, having given us beautiful conditions for our Qualifying Swim the day before. I like to think that we were doing what it took to swim the Channel and these gods were sending us affirming signs.

Although it had been extremely difficult, I am glad we did ten hours instead of six. The body and mind both start to react differently after six hours as hypothermia and fatigue begin to set in.

Later, I learned that almost all first-time Channel swimmers go through various forms of depression between the 6th and 8th hours of their swims. Accordingly, even though only six hours are required, I still recommend doing an eight to ten-hour cold water swim to prepare.

Ten hours also gave both Marcy and me an idea of our strengths and weaknesses. (And boy, did I discover mine!) During this time, the temptation to quit was enormous but some teeny tiny spirit within kept me going. I knew if I got out of the water, I might be at this same difficult point some time in the future; I wanted to get through it now. The strength of will I developed in Lake Sunapee helped me get through a lot of hard, laborious training in the coming months.

When I showed up at work the Monday after my Qualifying Swim, my boss noticed the tan line goggle marks around my eye sockets, my "raccoon eyes." He knew a lot about my long distance swimming but I hadn't yet told him of my English Channel aspiration. How was I to explain that I had swum for 10 hours in 60°F water "just for fun"? Instead, I explained, "I was out in the sun a little this weekend."

After my Qualifying Swim, I started to tell more of my family and friends about my plans to swim the English Channel. Reactions ranged from being extremely supportive to some people telling me that I was "totally crazy." After a while, instead of being offended by this latter response, I realized that these ego-centric people needed to level the playing field. In their own minds, they could never attempt to swim the Channel so they had to belittle my efforts for even trying. On the other hand, I really appreciated the supportive comments from sincere well-wishers.

FOUR

More Open Water Training

DURING THE FALL OF 1993, I CONTINUED to swim outdoors in Long Island Sound. Most of my swims were shorter (between one hour and one hour and 45 minutes) than during the previous fall. Robert was taking a break from swimming so I paired up with another swimmer. The lowest water temperature that fall was 52°F but I did not feel nearly as cold as I had the previous fall. I did not experience as much uncontrollable shaking and hypothermia that I did in 1992. Still, I was cold when I completed my last few swims, the final one being on November 7th, but my hands did not get as cramped as they had been the previous fall and it took me less time to warm up afterwards.

To get as much exposure as possible, I had decided to wear one latex bathing cap (in 1992, I had worn two) and my two-piece training bikini throughout the autumn. My training partner asked me at one point, "When are you going to start wearing a heavier suit and cap?" I responded flatly, "I'm not." (By then he was wearing a wet suit and two heavy caps!)

Just by chance the water conditions that fall were choppier and saltier than they had been the previous year. I built strength in the chop, and calluses from the salt rashes. Training in these conditions produced beneficial psychological and physiological changes. I developed an enormous amount of confidence and my body acclimated to the cold. A calm inner voice started to tell me, "You know you can do this because you've done it before. Just deal with it and take it as it comes. You'll be OK. Yes You Can."

Thoughts of how to keep myself warm prevailed. I could feel Mark's warm blanket hugs all around me. "Warm" songs played in my head. Billy Joel's album, "River of Dreams" had been released that summer and the title song went through my head over and over again, especially the lyrics:

And even though I know the river is wide
I walk down every evening and I stand on the shore
And try to cross to the opposite side
So I can finally find out what I've been looking for.

I would get into a swimming rhythm and just keep going, stroke after stroke, as this song played in my head. In hindsight, my acclimation that fall was amazing.

Gaining Weight

The rationale to weight gain is that a layer of subcutaneous fat helps to insulate the body against the cold water. The skin fat insulates, as does grease applied to a swimmer, or as a wetsuit would, although wetsuits are not permitted. Walruses do not seem to get cold because they wear their own internal wetsuits.

How much weight to gain was unclear. I could not find any guidelines. I just thought I should put on "a lot" of weight. Of the Channel swimmers I knew personally, the range was between 10 and 35 pounds.

In addition to its insulation value, body fat also adds buoyancy and provides a reserve of energy to draw on during prolonged strenuous effort. I intentionally gained about 20 pounds in ten months by eating everything I could get my hands on. By returning to my normal eating habits after my Channel swim, I lost all the excess weight in another ten months.

In retrospect, I think I could have swum the Channel as well or better if I had gained only five to eight pounds because the extra weight strained my stroke. Dragging those extra pounds around tired me out and made my joints hurt, both on land and in the water. I did not realize my acclimation would be such a major contributing factor. An irony seems to exist: the more weight you gain, the slower you go, which means you may be in the water longer, which makes you colder, so you need more body fat to stay warm.

Acclimation to the water temperature is the key. The more acclimated you are, the less weight you need to gain.

In the Spring of 1993, I had visited a nutritionist who helped me to get a handle on my eating habits. By eliminating sugar and wheat from my diet and eating more fruits, vegetables, and good-for-me food, I turned myself into a fit, lean machine. I felt terrific, visualizing that I was operating on all cylinders. In order to gain weight, I threw these great eating habits out the window and ate whatever I felt like eating. I would have felt better during my Channel training if I had filled up more on nuts, cheeses, and other nutritious snacks, rather than junk foods.

Breakfast usually consisted of oatmeal with butter, a roll or two with butter, maybe a doughnut after that, and then Ensure, a high calorie nutritional drink. Lunch was a sandwich or two, cookies, fruit, candy, and either a milkshake or a soda. More than once, I received incredulous stares from diners as they overheard me ordering lunch. I never shied away from an afternoon snack of whatever food in the vicinity was not nailed down. Dinner resembled a normal-sized meal but was usually followed by ice cream or another dessert. I estimate that I was eating between four- and five-thousand calories a day. For a while, it was actually fun but by the spring, all this face stuffing became more like a time-consuming job.

The women I swam with visually monitored my weight gain in the showers after swimming. Comments like, "It looks like you're putting it on evenly," were common. In actuality, I looked as if I had been hooked up to a helium pump and was slowly being inflated. Eventually some of my clothes no longer fit.

FIVE

Setting Training Goals

BY THE FALL OF 1993, I REALIZED THAT I needed to be swimming 45,000 yards per week in order to give myself sufficient endurance to tackle the Channel. Married and working full-time in an advertising sales job, I started to think of ways to break the 45,000 yards into manageable segments. I used lots of different types of sets and distances, including long straight freestyle swims, ladder sets, easy/fast with varying distances, sprints, kicking, stroke sets, and daily drills. I swam with a coached team, a small group, and also on my own. By this time, almost everyone knew about my goal and many of the workouts were constructed with long distance swimming in mind. I was committed to my training and I stuck to it.

In June 1993 I had begun to lift weights for the first time since college. Using Nautilus, Cybex, and free weights,

I went through a program twice a week which emphasized light to medium weights with high and/or multiple repetitions. Once in a while the weights felt too heavy so I would scale back. My objective was to build strength, not bulk since I didn't need to look as if I was ready for the Ms. Universe Contest. Including weight training as part of my overall preparation added to my strength, but I dreaded it towards the end. In June 1994, I promised myself that when this was over, I would never lift another weight in my life if I did not want to.

My usual training week went like this: On Monday and Tuesday, I would swim a total of at least 15,000 yards. On Wednesday and Thursday, I would try to repeat this distance and do the same again on Friday and Saturday, covering at least 45,000 yards every week. (Refer to Chart 1.) This allowed me to break up the total distance any way I wanted, making the mountains into just steep hills. Usually I swam 10,000 to 11,000 yards on Monday in morning and evening sessions with a team, then 4,000 to 5,000 yards at the Vanderbilt YMCA in Manhattan on Tuesday with a small group, after lifting weights on my own. I shot for 10,000 yards in two sessions on Wednesday, one session with a team and one with a group, then I usually swam 5,000 to 7,000 yards on my own on Thursday morning at the YMCA after lifting weights.

Friday was the swing day. If I had swum 39,000 yards by the end of my Friday morning session with the team,

CHART 1

WEEKLY TRAINING SCHEDULE

Session	MON	TUE	WED	THUR	FRI	SAT	SUN
Morning	A		A	C & D	A	A	OFF!
Noon		B & C	B		B (if necessary)		OFF!
Night	A						OFF!
Total Daily Yardage	10–11,000	4–5,000	10–11,000	5–7,000	5–10,000	6–7,000	
Total Cumulative Yardage	10–11,000	14–16,000	24–27,000	29–34,000	34–44,000	40–51,000	

A: Swim with a Team   **B:** Swim with a Small Group   **C:** Lift Weights   **D:** Swim on Own

then I didn't swim again on Friday since I would be able to get in 6,000 yards at Saturday morning's team practice. This became an enormous incentive to "front-end load" the week. I would usually take Sunday off. Both mental and physical rest are important. Whew!

Sometimes I rose to the challenges of training, sometimes not, but I always kept my eye on my long-range goal and completed the necessary yardage. During the past few years, I had worked my way up to swimming 2,000 to 3,000 yard sets at a pace of 1:15 per 100 yards. Some days I was more energetic than others, but it always bothered me if I couldn't make an interval, regardless of how tired I was. In the big picture it did not matter at all just as long as I was swimming the necessary yardage in a reasonable amount of time.

There was nothing melodramatic about my training. It was a means to an end, one stroke at a time. Either I did the work or I did not. It was completely my decision and whatever level of preparation I chose would either help me or haunt me later on in the English Channel.

When I swam at lunch time, I would walk hurriedly from my office to the Vanderbilt YMCA to prevent my brain from rationalizing what I was doing, and then swim at a fast pace in order to get back to work. The pace was set as I left my office and felt my feet moving quickly beneath me, and then felt my arms churn rapidly through my lunchtime workout. I dressed quickly, picked up a large lunch to eat at my desk and returned to my office for the afternoon's work, one more workout closer to my goal. On many days this whole training regimen felt like an "out of body experience," but it was also exciting. The process of swimming the Channel was coming together for me; I was making it happen each day and I was completely capable of stopping it at any moment. No one was forcing me to do this.

Incentive to Make it the First Time

It was difficult trying to cram everything into every day: marriage, work, swimming, maintaining our household, and planning for the Channel. This stress gave me a huge incentive to make it the first time; I did not want to go through this again.

I love my husband, Mark and the life we have together. During this whole Channel process, we made sure we had time together; my swimming could never be more important than our marriage. He has always been very supportive of my life pursuits. Each week I spelled out to Mark what the upcoming week looked like, training and work-wise. Fortunately, he loves to read so he often filled my long hours away with reading time. He also understood my commitment to this goal and could see that I was approaching it whole-heartedly. One of the reasons I put so much emphasis on being efficient during my own training time was so Mark and I could have time together.

To know I had a specific goal made the necessary diligence easier. Every day I successfully completed my daily goals meant that I was one day closer to my goal. I had the necessary mind set, the "Channel Focus."

Unwavering Discipline

Long ago, my parents and my age group swim coaches had helped me to develop an unwavering sense of discipline which I expanded upon during my Channel preparation. Big goals are achievable, especially when they are broken down into reasonable pieces. The challenging part was maintaining the consistency when it would be easy to do otherwise. Swimming the English Channel is a lengthy process, not a one-day event.

There were times when training was challenging to me but I tried to maintain a positive attitude. There were days when I didn't feel like training but I did it anyway. It would have been very easy to back off from the discomfort and responsibility of such intense training but my goal was important to me and I hung in there. A friend said after my Channel swim, "Pain might not be fun but it isn't necessarily bad."

It would also have been easier *not* to try than to try and fail. But I wanted to fulfill my potential and not wonder, "What if?"

The intense training I did from September 1993 to July 1994 is what got me across the English Channel. When I reflect upon how I did it, the response is always the same, "One stroke at a time."

SIX

Mental Transformation

THE WINTER OF 1994 IN THE NORTHEAST
United States proved to be one of the most severe in recent
memory. Seventeen snowstorms in four months dumped
several feet of snow on New York City. When I took the
bus to the Vanderbilt YMCA on Thursday mornings, I
would often wait in snowy darkness, in view of an outdoor
thermometer which usually read 20°F. I inwardly wondered,
"Why are you subjecting yourself to this?" and "Is this all
going to work out?"

To answer the first question: I was subjecting myself to
these regimens because I wanted to be successful; and, in
fact, it *was* all worth it. I knew I wanted to be successful;
it was the price I felt I had to pay. I was both prisoner and
warden of this project.

To answer the second question: I had no idea if
everything was going to work out. These training memories
were some of the things I was able to reflect upon at the

start of my Channel swim. The difficult part was behind me, albeit at a high cost, and I felt I had earned a fair shot at a good Channel swim. I paid my dues and I owed it to myself to give it my best shot.

BREAKTHROUGH

Suddenly, swimming 6,000 to 7,000 yards before work did not seem so taxing anymore, physically or mentally. I got to the point where I could often do this much in one straight swim, even after lifting weights.

These long swims gave me time to think. I thought about the concept of suffering and at what point would I give up? My Qualifying Swim had been a good first test. Often I asked myself, "When things get *really* bad, am I willing to stick it out?"

Sometimes we forget about the process leading to success and focus only on the final outcome. Our society has done much to eliminate suffering from daily life. At the slightest discomfort, we often back off instead of forging ahead. Preparing to swim the English Channel made me face many challenges. Some I confronted, and some I backed away from. Ultimately I would have to live with myself if I gave up knowing that I could have gone on. As my ability slowly solidified my will, a realization crystallized: nothing great is easy.

During this whole process I was acutely aware that, while other people were helpful and supportive, the outcome of my Channel swim was solely my responsibility.

Becky—Another Training Partner

Swimming with different groups in different pools added variety to what otherwise could have become drudgery. The weekly swim I looked forward to most was Thursday morning at the Vanderbilt YMCA with Becky Fenson. Becky was training for the August 1994 Manhattan Island Marathon Swim (281/2 miles around Manhattan). I loved to swim with her. She was thoughtful, well-organized, inspiring, and had a wonderful sense of energy. We fed each other lots of training ideas, and motivational cues, and continually dealt with delayed gratification. It was a godsend to be around someone with an unwavering, focused approach to achieving a goal. Her enthusiasm for cranking out the fast yardage kept me motivated through many lulls. Even when we were not swimming together, knowing that Becky was doing a similar long and challenging workout helped me to cope with what I was doing. Becky was the fastest American to swim the English Channel in 1996: in 10 hours, 12 minutes.

CONQUERING "FATIGUE MOUNTAIN"

That spring I coined the phrase "Channel Tired" because rarely in my life had I ever been so tired. Combining working full time with swimming 25 miles a week, lifting weights twice a week, and running a few times a week took its toll. Although I still got up at 5 a.m. every weekday to train before work, my usual 9:30 p.m. bedtime started creeping back to 9 p.m. By April/May, I would often fall asleep around 8:30 p.m. and learned to sleep with the lights and television on since Mark stayed up later. A few times my speech even became tongue-tied because I was so tired. Somehow I dragged myself around through life and training, never losing sight of my long range goal.

I started to deal better with swimming 45,000 yards a week but there were a lot of plateaus. In September 1993, coming off my open water season, I could easily hold a pace of 1 minute 12 seconds per 100 yards for an hour. By mid-January, I struggled with 1 minute 15 seconds for my 100 yard pace. My arms felt like lead and I kept thinking, "This is how I will feel in the tenth or eleventh hour of my Channel swim." I kept going since I was just tired, not in pain.

Gauges of Fatigue

In January 1994 I did three long swims for distance that were good indicators of my training. In a relaxed two-hour swim on January 2nd, I covered 9,200 yards with 30 second stops every half-hour for drinks and stretching. This works out to a pace a little faster than 1 minute 18 seconds per 100 yards. During the next week, I did a set of four 2,000 yard swims at an interval of 1 minute 15 seconds per 100 yards. At the end of the month, I participated in the annual National One Hour Swim, covering 4,900 yards at a pace of 1 minute 13 seconds per 100 yards. I had swum exactly the same amount on my way to a 6,000 yard swim in November 1993, but now I was a few pounds heavier.

During one week in February 1994, I could barely hold a pace of 1 minute 18 seconds for 100 yards freestyle even though I was really trying, and I felt quite discouraged. But two days later in practice, I swam a negative split 400 yard butterfly in 5 minutes 23 seconds (splits: 2:46, 2:37). That is, I swam the second half (the last 200 yards) faster than the first half of a long swim in the most strenuous stroke! Where did I find the energy to do this? It seemed that I was constantly on one side or the other of "Fatigue Mountain."

In May 1994, I spoke with Sharon Beckman, an American woman who had swum the Channel in 1982 in 9 hours and 6 minutes. I read about her in a Channel article and happened to see one of her crew members at a swim meet in early May. When I described my training to her, Sharon was very reassuring, commenting, "It sounds as if you're where you should be." Our approach to training and our ability levels were similar, and she also had experienced the same level of fatigue I had.

Interestingly, by June 1994, just before I left for my three week "training camp" in Maine, I was back to a pace of 1 minute and 12 seconds for 100 yards, despite the fact that I was 15 pounds heavier than the previous September. The nervous energy combined with the sense of imminence helped propel me. Things were coming to a head. Then, in Maine, I had three solid weeks of training and feeling good in the water.

LONG POOL SWIMS

In February and March 1994, I did three longer pool swims for time in a 50 meter pool. (A 50 meter pool is approximately 55 yards long.) Going into each of these long swims all clocks were moved out of my range of vision and I only had a vague idea of how long I would be in the water. Someone would simply tell me when to stop, sometime between three and six hours. It was going to take as long as it was going to take.

I hated each one of these long pool swims but I learned a lot about myself. I am not very good at surrendering control, especially when it comes to time, but I had no choice during these swims. The point was to break my self-imposed mental time limits. If I had decided before my Channel attempt that I could only swim for a certain amount of time and I surpassed that time, would I be able to continue? By having no idea how long I was swimming, I was forced to just keep going. Anyway, the pool was only three feet deep so if I started to go down, someone would come in and get me. (I'm an optimist.) Physically, I was fine on all these swims.

The stress of sensory deprivation from being in the same unchanging environment for such a long time was hard for me. I had to figure out ways to entertain myself. People on the pool deck would occasionally come and go which does not sound that interesting but when everything else remains the same, trying to figure out what they were doing alleviated some of my boredom. I was told that the scenery in the English Channel was pretty constant for all but the first and last hours: water, the escort boat, the horizon, and the next stroke. As dull as it was, this sensory deprivation practice proved invaluable.

These swims also helped build my endurance. During the course of a multiple hour swim, I was swimming about 4,000 meters (4400 yards) per hour, thus adding to my weekly yardage base. Doing long, straight swims allowed my body to get into a constant rhythm that I usually could not achieve in my regular workouts. Whenever I did a long swim I skipped my regular Saturday workout.

My longest pool swim was 5 hours and 4 minutes. Frankly, I would now recommend only a four hour pool swim if there is consistent access to open water; long open water swims are far more important. But during all of my long pool swims, I did not whine, cry or beg to get out. It wouldn't have mattered if I did. Except for when I stopped for my feedings, I just kept swimming even though it was monotonous and boring. Mark kept track of the time (along with a few others) and he decided when I would stop. It was extremely hard for me to have someone else in control of my swimming but this is a "Channel Reality." The Channel decides when you are through. You just keep going until you can't go any further. Stopping to complain just lengthens the time you swim.

The "bellies" of my biceps usually tired after three hours during these long swims, but I discovered a high carbohydrate drink that helped enormously. To combat the monotony and boredom, I would toss my head around a lot, like a horse trying to lose its bit. This threw my stroke off, made me tired and dizzy, and was completely counter-productive – I was told to knock it off. I also sang songs to myself, counted the number of strokes I took each lap, and tried to figure out what was going on in the surrounding pool area. Becky and a few other swimmers would sometimes join me during these swims. It was nice to have company because I became really bored.

Afterwards, as much as I disliked these long swims, I did experience a sense of weary accomplishment. I was cold, achy, and parched, and my exhausted senses were overloaded with the aroma of chlorine, but I could look back and know what I had done. The feelings of being thoroughly worn out and completely drained were stepping stones towards my Channel swim, part of the overall process.

I found that if I had a massage the day after a long swim and took Motrin, I recovered faster. During my year of intensive training for the Channel, I got a massage every other week.

Another significant reason for these long swims was to determine my reaction to various foods. Some foods made me feel sick to my stomach and some gave me an energy boost; my reaction was all over the map. But the important thing was to test different foods so that when it came to the "real thing" I would be firing on all cylinders. The middle of the English Channel is not the place to be experimenting with food combinations.

I discovered during my long open water swims that my system reacted differently in salt water than in a chlorinated pool so I tested my Channel foods in salt water as well.

Switching Metabolic Systems

During the winter, I spoke to Mike Oram twice on the phone. In one of these conversations, he suggested that I go into my long pool swims on an empty stomach so my body would learn how to burn fat effectively. Since I did not eat before my morning workouts I was already doing this, thus simulating the physiological condition after swimming for a few hours. My system was already learning to switch over from its initial stores of carbohydrates and glycogen to fats right from the start of a swim.

Mike Oram also made several suggestions about training, including, what he called, "Total Body Confusion Training," such as swimming 1/2 hour one day and three hours the next. "Your body shouldn't recognize the difference. The first hour should feel like the tenth." (I didn't do this, but it is an excellent idea.)

He suggested that I practice taxing myself mentally by extending a swim for another one, two, three, etc. hours, but not deciding until the middle of the swim. "You decide. Push yourself another hour or more because the biggest reason why swimmers get out is that they just give up."

Green Light for the Summer

On a Friday afternoon in February 1994, my boss and my supervisor came into my office with good news. A three-week leave of absence followed by three consecutive weeks of vacation had been approved by management, just as long as "we didn't miss a beat" on any of my sales accounts. I was thrilled and relieved to have the support of my employer behind my Channel effort.

Just before I left, the national director of the company said, "I wish more people here had personal goals like yours."

➤ 25 Kilometer Race at Wrightsville Beach

Warm-up for the Channel

I thought swimming in the 1994 United States Swimming National 25 Kilometer Championship (15 1/2 miles) on

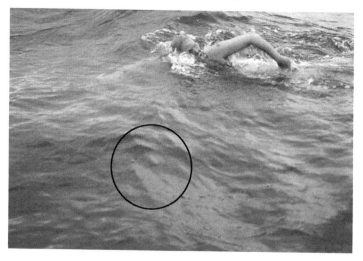

Battling the elements at Wrightsville Beach, June 11, 1994. The circle shows one of the many stinging jellyfish in the water that day.

June 11th would be a good warm-up for the Channel. The top two finishers in this race would qualify to represent the United States at the World Swimming Championship in Rome that August. Consequently, all the "big guns" in United States long distance swimming were there. In my wildest fantasy, I would do well and represent the USA in Rome. In reality, I did not have a prayer of placing and would be very happy with simply finishing. I was there for the experience.

The race was held in the Atlantic Ocean at Wrightsville Beach, North Carolina. The seas were running four to six feet on race day. UGH! To give the ocean a chance to calm down, the race director even postponed the starting time an hour. The cloudy skies kept spitting rain all day and the wind was hard at work.

One of the turning buoys at Wrightsville Beach. Quite a rough day!

There were 30 competitors. We were told to enter the stormy water and swim 75 yards off shore to the starting line. I had never felt such anxiety before a race. It was not that I doubted my ability to swim the distance; it was the rough conditions that frightened me. To complicate matters, the water was laced with stinging jellyfish. As everyone started to lunge through the waves, I badly wanted to run back to the beach, to the comfort of dry land. I was shaking with fear but rationalized, "If these 29 other people are going to try, I can too." I had made the time and financial commitment to be there so I simply had to move forward. Also, Mark had taken time off from work to be there with me. I would have felt enormously guilty if I had quit before the start.

The triangular course went south along the beach for two miles, took a left turn, veered northeast out into the rough Atlantic Ocean for four miles, then headed back two miles towards the beach and the starting point. Two loops of this course equaled 25 kilometers (15 1/2 miles). When the starting gun went off I thought if I could just swim to my escort boat a mile away I would be ok. About five minutes later I thought, "It would be enough if I could just complete one loop of this course."

I had never failed to finish a race before. I knew that the English Channel lay on the horizon for me and beating myself up before that swim hardly made sense.

A few minutes later, with overwhelming relief, I spotted Mark in the tiny escort boat assigned to me. I was so happy to see him and knew I would be ok now. Mark is a pretty good swimmer but when I saw he was wearing a life preserver my heart sank and I realized the severity of the seas. At the first feeding stop I told the crew about my "one loop" goal. No one challenged it.

When I finally did get out after seven miles (seven miles across the ocean and about three miles up and down) in 3 hours and 10 minutes, I had gained the experience of dealing with rough seas, numerous jellyfish stings, queasiness, overall discomfort, and the disappointment of not finishing a race. At least I had tried. I found out later that several swimmers had left the race before me, including some world class marathon swimmers.

Lisa Hazen finished fourth in the race which impressed me because we were both 30 years old. We had discussed feedings before the race and she mentioned her mixture of liquid carbohydrates and skim milk for protein. I thought that sounded gross, but I was intrigued by the idea of adding protein to a carbohydrate mix for a long swim. When I got home I bought some vanilla-flavored protein powder. Mixed with my carbohydrate drink, it went down like a watery vanilla milkshake and provided some extra firepower when I used it during my Channel swim.

SEVEN

Maine

BEFORE I LEFT FOR ENGLAND, I SET UP a three week "training camp" for myself in Maine. Through this whole process I had wondered how I would do if I temporarily focused my life primarily on swimming. Being in Maine afforded me this opportunity. A friend had suggested that the Harpswell area would be ideal. It was. Situated on the southern coast of Maine near Brunswick, I had the chance to swim in cold water every day during my stay, focusing on my upcoming Channel swim, and honing in on what worked for me. For the first time in a long, long time, I was able to sort things out, mentally and physically, without the usual distractions of day-to-day life.

This was a wonderful time in my life and I am thankful for the experience. Being in Maine before my Channel swim made the difference for me between "just" crossing the Channel and swimming it as well as I did.

SELECTING A CREW

It is important to select a crew well ahead of a planned Channel swim. Crew members need to practice their roles and adjust their lives and work schedules to suit the swimmer. There are no hard and fast rules for selecting a crew. The Handbook only indicates that you must have at least a trainer. I wanted three people for assistance although ultimately I would do my swim with two. I wanted people who knew me well and could deal with the stresses of a Channel swim, such as weather, fatigue (both theirs and mine), and seasickness. I was looking for people who were dependable, conscientious and caring, but who could order me around if I got tired and cranky. They also had to follow a few rules: no cold water jokes, no shark jokes, and don't ask me if I'm tired.

Mark, of course, was my first choice and would be my officially appointed trainer. I had also asked two friends whom I swam with in New York and both had agreed to go. They had a good handle on my training and swimming ability and would have principal roles in my Channel swim. In the beginning of June, just six weeks before I left for England, these two quit!

As much of a shock as it was at the time, and then a scramble to find replacements, everything happened for the best. When I told Mark about my crew situation, he said with calm resolve, "Now I'm in charge," realizing the full responsibility he was assuming. A friend told me at one difficult time, "Use what you got," and I truly did.

Mark knew how to direct a crew, having gone from a novice to an expert in the past few years. As much as I was preparing for the Channel in the water, Mark prepared for it as a crew member. Through careful observation he learned to anticipate and respond to my needs. Most importantly, I trusted him completely. He knew what my goals were and he had been through lots of hard swims with me.

One of Mark's close friends from college, Terry Tyner, was available to be part of our Channel crew and quickly proved himself to be invaluable. Even though Terry's swimming background was limited, he is one of our most supportive and helpful friends. He came to Maine and crewed for me on several swims with Mark, immediately catching on to the responsibilities involved. He also arranged to take two weeks vacation from his job to go to England with us. The competent combination of Mark and Terry had a great deal to do with my success.

Training Tricks in Maine

We rented a three-bedroom ranch house on Orr's Island, just outside of Brunswick, Maine. I swam for an hour every morning, Monday to Friday, at the beautiful Bowdoin College pool, working on drills, kicking, stroke, and sprints. After my pool session, I swam for two to three hours in open water alongside Bailey Island where the water temperature ranged between 56°F and 61°F. On two consecutive Saturdays, I did longer open water swims, between 3 1/2 and 7 1/2 hours. On Sundays, I rested.

Armed with the knowledge I had gained through reading, experience, and from previously being coached by some excellent people, the training I assigned to myself was consistently hard. I developed a pace that was not fatiguing, something I called my "forever pace." A rate of 72 to 76 strokes per minute felt comfortable for hours and by swimming so often in open water, I developed a longer, rolling stroke. In fact, after my 7 1/2 hour swim, I hopped out of the water feeling fine, showered, cleaned up the day's gear, and was eating dinner in a restaurant within an hour, just like a 'normal' person.

My training in Maine was the first time in my life I swam alone for an extended period of time with no training partner or coach. I learned to trust my own judgment to prepare myself for the great adventure in England, and definitely benefited from having time alone to focus. *I was the only person who could get inside my mind and body to figure out what was best for me.* There were other swimmers at Bowdoin so I was not swimming in isolation, and I always swam with a piloted boat when I was in the open water. But I designed my own workouts and learned to make stroke adjustments by feel.

One of the drills I invented in Maine I call "Pick Ups." When I was training there, I always swam at a medium to fast speed, never allowing myself the luxury of easing back. But every 30 minutes, I would throw in an all-out five minute "sprint" at 80 to 86 strokes per minute. These Pick Ups usually came right before a feeding regardless of the water conditions. They were excellent preparation for my Channel swim because they forced me to increase my speed by turning my arms over more quickly. Whoever was in the boat noted my stroke rate about every five minutes when I was not sprinting and about every minute during the Pick Ups. They would write my stroke rate on the grease board for me to see; of course, I was always looking to better what I had done before. These Pick Ups were demanding and I could not fake them. Five minutes is a long time when you're going all out and being closely monitored. I dreaded seeing the grease board sign, "sprint." While I was training in Maine, I had no idea how helpful these Pick Ups would soon be.

In Maine I was very hard on myself, fully aware that I was there for a purpose, not a vacation. My training distance increased to about 80,000 yards a week (46 miles), yet I felt less tired than I had in New York. Weekly massages also helped.

Surprising Myself

In 1978, Penny Dean, an American woman, established a world record for the English Channel with a time of seven hours, forty minutes. She is an obvious authority and has written a superb book, *Open Water Swimming*, published in 1998, as well as *The United States Swimming Long Distance Training Manual*, published in 1992. Before I went to Maine, I blanched at some of her training suggestions. During my last week in Maine, when I read them again, I realized I had exceeded many of them without specifically planning to do so. I don't think I could have done this while working full time at my advertising sales job. My mental preparation was becoming fine-tuned and I was getting psyched about swimming the Channel by training in Channel-like conditions every day. The anticipation kept me moving forward at a very quick pace and helped me stay energized.

Touch of Reality

I kept in touch with my office job even though I was on a leave of absence, receiving electronic mail through my computer, regular mail via Federal Express, and calling in every day. My clients occasionally called me to discuss business. It was good to have a bit of my other world.

Parental Involvement

During the first two weeks of my training my parents accompanied me in the boat during my open water swims. My father was with me during the first week and my mother was there for the second. They kept a log of each swim which included my stroke rate, the water and air conditions, feedings and my physical and mental states.

Because they were with me all day and all night either in our rented house or in the boat, my parents had a window into the unglamorous life of a marathon swimmer. They witnessed first hand the necessary tough training which gave them a better understanding of my diligence and determination to succeed.

I braved the cold water day after day without complaining; I swam head-on into waves, seaweed, and choppy seas. I dealt with aches, pains, salt rashes, suit rubs, and general muscle fatigue, all with a smile. At times, the water was so rough that my arms would be literally blown backwards and waves would break over me. My parents could see that this was hard work and there weren't any shortcuts.

LIFE IN MAINE

Thursday June 23rd

I left New York City for Maine on Thursday June 23rd, 1994. Mark and I woke up at 5:30 a.m. that morning and packed the car. Mark then waved good-bye and headed off to work. I was on the road before 7AM with the feeling that I was on an important mission.

Friday June 24th

After spending the previous night at my sister's house in Massachusetts, I arrived on Bailey Island, Maine, around lunch time. I stopped by the realtor's office, completed the necessary paperwork, and headed over to what would become the headquarters for my training camp. I unpacked the car, set up the house, and had just enough time to get to the Portland Airport to pick up Mark at 8 p.m.. During my time in Maine, I was always so relieved and happy to see him every weekend even though we talked on the phone several times a day. He is a solid fixture in my life, and even as exciting and different as my life was during this time, the "constants" helped to keep me grounded.

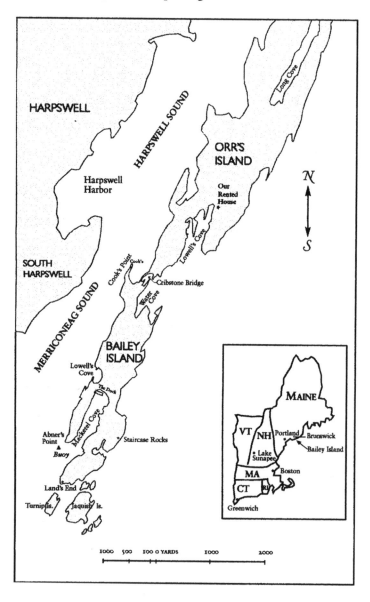

First Maine Training Day: Saturday June 25th

The weather was rotten: very foggy and damp, a typical early summer day in Maine. The air and the water felt raw (both were about 60°F) and I dreaded jumping into the ink-black water. Mark and I hung around most of the morning, putting off the inevitable. In the early afternoon, we went to the dock at Mackerel Cove to meet Josh Allen, a local 13-year-old, whom I had hired for the next three weeks to accompany me in his small boat during my open water swims. The realtor who rented us the house in Maine recommended Josh, and the recommendation was well-deserved; Josh was a very capable skipper and his deft control, maturity and wisdom far surpassed his years.

We hopped in Josh's boat and motored the three-quarters of a mile to Abner's Point at the end of Mackerel Cove to check out the area and further delay the inevitable swim. The Cove was surrounded by high, rocky cliffs that plunged straight down into dark water. By the end of my stint in Maine, I would be sorry to leave these beautiful waters but on Day One, I was scared to enter them. Everything looked so ominous. I had not swum since Wednesday morning. What was one more day? These were not the rational thoughts of a confident Channel swimmer.

Sunday June 26th—Getting In

Ronnie Kamphausen, a swimmer friend from Connecticut, spends her summers in Maine and had given me her phone number in case I wanted to get together. Boy, did I need help! I called her on Saturday night and we made a swim date for Sunday morning. Swimming with someone else is always comforting and Ronnie helped me "break the ice" into the Maine waters.

Mark and I drove to Ronnie's house on Sunday morning and followed her to a state park nearby. Although the sun

Josh Allen, the 13-year-old who skippered for me in Maine.

was sparkling on the water, it was windy. The spot where we were swimming was protected from the open Atlantic Ocean by only a couple of large rocks and the water was 54°F. Ronnie donned her wetsuit and I put on my usual outfit of suit, cap, and goggles and waded in. OUCH! I was freezing! The only way to become unfrozen was to sprint and I did so immediately. As icy as it was, it was also incredibly beautiful. The crystal clear water allowed me to see the boulders and tiny fish along the bottom. They probably wondered what those crazy humans were doing up

Beautiful Mackerel Cove! The boat dock is on the far right.

there on the surface. We did laps parallel to the beach for 40 minutes. I shivered for a while when I got out but at least I had completed my first swim.

Sunday June 26th—Evening

It was time for Mark to return to New York and his job; he would return to Maine every weekend. After taking him to the airport I knew I was now completely on my own and I was scared. There was no one for me to rely on, and being alone in a house in an unfamiliar area with hard training coming up overwhelmed me at the time. Mark called later that night to let me know he had gotten home safely. Eventually I fell into a fitful sleep and woke up tired the next morning. I had a big challenge in front of me and I needed to take this one stroke at a time.

Monday June 27th: The Three Week Plan

This was my first full day alone in Maine. My father would arrive that evening. I thought, "Gee, I could sit on the couch for three weeks and eat Bon Bons since nobody is watching over me or making me swim."

No way! I was there for a purpose and I wanted to make the most of every minute.

Here at last: my first real training day. I told Josh I wanted to swim some place calm. Josh and his friend, Jason, took me to Lowell Cove where the water was 58°F. When I first jumped in the two boys got really excited, waving their arms and pointing at me. I stopped swimming and asked them what was going on. They exclaimed, "You're so fast!"

I guess they had never seen a 'real' swimmer before. I did a few laps around the perimeter of Lowell Cove and then got brave: I turned the corner and went out into Merriconeag Sound, which flows into Casco Bay. A wall of 56°F water hit me, but I continued to swim away from the Cove and alongside Bailey Island for a bit before coming back to the Cove. This frigid little excursion made the 58°F Cove water seem welcoming. In an hour I did two more similar laps and then climbed into the boat. The introduction was over.

One of the deceptive things about open water is the temperature changes. There are often upwellings of warmer or colder water, spots where the water coming up from the bottom can be a few (or more!) degrees colder or warmer than the surface water temperature. You never know where these pockets are until you enter them. If they're warmer you don't want to leave, but more than likely they are colder, making you want to move on as quickly as possible.

I thrive on structure. While in Maine, I set my alarm for 5:30 a.m. every weekday morning, but I was often awake before 5 a.m. and lay in bed thinking about what was coming up that day. I would stretch for about half an hour while watching the news on television, then eat breakfast, and leave at 6:30 a.m. for the 20 minute drive to the Bowdoin pool. During my first week, after swimming for an hour, I would head home for another breakfast then swim outdoors with Josh later in the day. During the second and third weeks I ate breakfast in the car as I headed straight to the dock after Bowdoin for my open water swim of the day with Josh. Afterwards I would shower and eat a big lunch, followed by a snack, dinner and then, often, another snack. I was consuming about 5,000 calories a day, including two bowls of ice cream!

Tuesday June 27th and Wednesday June 28th

The next day, with Josh and my father, I went to Water Cove, on the other side of the Cribstone Bridge. The water was 59°F and I stayed in for 1½ hours. The cold water did not affect me at all. The day after that the weather was very foggy so, to be safe, I swam for two hours in Mackerel Cove where the water was 57°F.

This swim was hard because it was not sunny and my toes got very cold. (The sun makes such a difference.) The second hour was pretty unpleasant but I never got to the point where I could not go on. That day I was experimenting with a different bathing suit and it was giving me a bad suit rub.

Many of my flashcard sayings came to mind during these two hours, especially about how I had to earn it. Several conditions of this swim, when both the water and the air were cold, when a lot of things were making me uncomfortable and I was not complaining, were all elements of "earning it."

The Next Two Weeks

Around this time I started thinking of my time in Maine on a week-by-week basis instead of day-by-day, and what would be the most effective training plan for each week. After this swim in Mackerel Cove I started doing two-mile laps alongside Bailey Island, from Abner's Point to Cook's Restaurant and back. This became my standard route unless the weather was bad. If it was, I was confined to Mackerel Cove because it would not be safe for either Josh or me to be in a less protected area.

Life on Shore

The people in Maine were a wonderful, wholesome lot. The Harpswell community is a tight-knit, hardworking, industrious group, happily self-sufficient, the type of folks who pack their own parachutes. You are only considered a native if you were born on the island. (While in Maine, I met a grandmother who had lived there since the early 1950's and did not consider herself a native.) Word travels fast and all the locals seem to know the current news, such as who was the woman swimming in Merriconeag Sound every day and why she was there. By the second week people living in houses overlooking the Sound started noticing that "someone is swimming out there." By the third week they were watching and waving and I waved back! An insider's loop very much exists on Bailey Island.

Later when I met Josh's grandfather, Bruce Allen, he told me that he had watched me from his house overlooking Mackerel Cove. He had remarked many times while I swam, "This is definitely it," meaning that this lap would be my last because of the fast speed at which he thought I was swimming. He would be amazed to see me turn and do several more laps at the same speed, saying the same thing to himself as I neared the end of each lap.

Depending on the tide and the wind, the current was usually strong in one direction. That meant one way was relatively easy and the other was challenging: waves and wind hitting both me and the skiff head on. My father and mother each spent days in Josh's skiff, after which I seemed to be drier than they were. The regular two to three foot waves made monitoring a swim an athletic feat in itself!

These conditions were perfect Channel preparation. Swimming against the current through heavy, choppy seas made me physically and mentally strong. The only time I ever cut a corner during any of my training was during a two hour swim in the second week when my mother had been thoroughly drenched by the waves and it was not going to make any difference to my conditioning whether or not I swam for another 15 minutes. So I got out. Mom is still drying off!

The water in Merriconeag Sound was clean and clear and the craggy cliffs lining the shoreline offered a spectacular view. The water often smelled like fresh fish even though I only saw about a dozen fish during all my swims. Occasionally I ran into some minor vegetation but the only real obstacles I had to watch out for were the omnipresent lobster pot buoys. Josh did a good job steering me around them and in our three weeks together Josh and I only hit one each.

Equipment Testing

During the first two weeks I tested several different bathing suits and caps to determine which ones chafed and where. Suits with skinny straps worked best for me since they didn't chafe my neck or armpits. Heavier bathing caps (the type 'old ladies' wear when they swim, complete with chin straps) chafed at the nape of my neck. Mark solved the problem with a pair of shaving clippers, trimming all hair in this area.

A Final Acclimation Occurs

It amazed me to see how my body adapted to this intense cold water training; it no longer exhausted me. I slept well at night. I remember taking only one or two cat naps during my entire time in Maine, both during the first week. In a way I was psychologically challenging myself to get by on whatever sleep I had at night, knowing that I might not get a whole lot of sleep the night before my Channel swim.

I was also challenging myself physiologically. By the middle of the second week, 58°F to 60°F water felt comfortable so I started to wear my training bikini during outdoor swims to get as much exposure to the cold water as possible. After my swims I intentionally took only cold showers. I had no idea just how well acclimated I had become.

One day Mark and I discovered the Staircase Rocks. Thin slabs of indigenous rock had been up-ended, creating log- and stair-like steps with a meditative appeal. We would walk down as many stairs as the tide would allow and look out over the expansive ocean. Amazingly, this view turned out to resemble the English Channel closely. From here I visualized a slow moving boat escorting a swimmer. We visited this place of contemplation often, both with friends and by ourselves.

LONG SWIMS

While I was in Maine, I planned to do two longer swims, both on weekends when Mark would be with me. One would be between three and four hours and the second between seven and eight hours.

During these swims, I wore just a regular one-piece lycra suit (the one I eventually wore during my Channel swim) and a latex cap, and applied Vaseline only where I knew I might get suit rubs. The more exposed I allowed myself to be in the cold water, the better acclimated I would be for the Channel.

Like my long pool swims, I would not have precise control over the length of these swims; Mark would decide how long each one would be, based on my condition, the water conditions, and whatever he felt like doing. I figured if I was "well-behaved" and did not complain or ask how much longer, and did my sprints as requested, I would get off early for good behavior. Wrong!

First Long Swim

This swim took place at the end of my first week in Maine. Mark and Terry had come up for the long July 4th weekend. Josh planned to call me on Saturday morning so we could arrange a meeting time for that afternoon. In any case, I had all the equipment ready to go the day before. When the phone rang around 8 a.m., Josh wanted to know if I could go right then. Since it was his boat and I was up there to swim, we quickly gathered everything together, poured hot water directly from the tap into the thermoses and headed to the dock. I actually prefer to swim in the morning but it was somewhere between amusing and annoying to be abiding by the last minute planning of a 13-year-old.

It was a clear but windy day and the air temperature hovered near 80°F. I entered the 59°F water just before 10 a.m., knowing that four hours of swimming lay in front of me. Most people would question my sanity but I was actually looking forward to it. It was a nice day, the water conditions were good (just some minor chop in one direction), and Mark and Terry were crewing for me. I was doing something I loved and working hard at it.

As usual, I jumped off the boat at Abner's Point and eventually swam more than two full loops from there to Cook's and back. Terry instituted Pick Ups for the five minutes before all my half-hour feedings. I had to go all out since he would measure my effort by my stroke rate, which went from between a steady 68 to 72 strokes a minute to a rapid-fire 80 strokes per minute.

Mark gave me combinations of Fig Newtons, bananas, a carbohydrate drink, and tea at the feedings. The foods that went down easiest and proved to be the most effective for my energy level would go to England. These feedings were intended to be dress rehearsals for the "real thing," hence they had to be fast. All of them were well under a minute, during which I consumed my food, stretched, communicated with the boat about how I felt and what our immediate plans were, then resumed swimming. All other communication had to take place using the grease board or hand-signals. No dilly-dallying here or in the Channel.

It took me about an hour to feel the three Cs in the water: calm, confident and comfortable. The day before the local grapevine murmured, "The blues are running," indicating that bluefish were in the area. If a school gets into a feeding frenzy, bluefish will eat whatever is in their path; I was thinking this might be me. Although I never had a problem the entire time I was in Maine, I worried about "the blues running" during this swim and wanted the boat right next to me. So much for the brave Channel swimmer.

After an hour, I felt more relaxed. I was always able to crank it out for those Pick Ups and in good enough shape so I could recover easily. Changing speed alleviated some of the monotony that sets in when one has been doing the same thing over and over again.

Just after this first hour, Mark noticed my fingers spreading out a bit, one of the initial signs of hypothermia, a result of the many cold upwellings I had encountered that day. Mark also noticed that my stroke looked less deliberate and was a bit sloppier than it had been at the start, even though my stroke rate remained constant. A few moments later I regained my form but my left hand continued to look slightly cramped and gnarled most of the day.

I estimated that if it took about two hours for a round trip from Abner's Point, I would pass that spot at least twice. The Calculation Queen hard at work! On my second return trip, more than half way there, Mark signaled, "That's it! You're done!" It was three hours and 34 minutes into the swim. I climbed into the boat and we were all back on terra firma soon.

My lower back and left shoulder hurt a little afterwards, making me re-evaluate my plans for pain relief. During this swim, the pain had been somewhat lessened by hourly doses of Liquid Tylenol (Acetaminophen). I decided for my next long swim to take a Motrin (Ibuprofen) before the start and then another at six hours. That should suffice. Such medicines are allowed by the organizing bodies of Channel Swimming. *(Before a swim, it is best to confirm with the organization with which you are swimming about what medicines are permissible.)*

Two of the casualties of that swim were my lips and tongue. They became very swollen from the salt water even though Mark had put Vaseline on lemon wedges for me to suck during my feedings. This swelling is simply one of those side effects of submerging one's mouth in salt water for an extended period of time. Since my swim, I have come to the conclusion that lemons are a waste of time. Putting lots of Vaseline on the inside of the feeding cup, opposite the drinking side, works better. Later I discovered that rinsing with mouthwash at the end of a feeding works best.

I was fairly comfortable during that long swim and felt as though I could always keep moving forward. The water temperature was not a factor and the frequent sprints helped to warm me up. Terry was great at keeping me informed with what I needed to know, writing messages on the grease board. The jokes often made me laugh. And even though I knew I would see the dreaded "SPRINT" sign every half-hour, I secretly loved it.

That swim helped my confidence a great deal; I bounced back from it with very little fatigue. I realized that being in Maine, where I was able to relax and focus on training, helped enormously. After swimming more than 80,000 yards a week I did not feel exhausted; instead, I felt great.

Second Long Swim

I did my second long swim on Saturday, July 9th. This was going to be a long day, and we all knew it ahead of time. Our friends, Dana and David, had come up from Manhattan for the weekend. I had known Dana since 1988 when we started swimming together in New York; Dana and David have been partners since 1981. They were terrific in every way, as crew members on my 7 1/2 hour swim and keeping everyone entertained in the boat with their non-stop humorous banter. As with the previous long swim, Mark would decide the length of time I swam.

Josh and I arranged to meet at the dock at 8:30a.m. since I wanted to be in the water by 9 a.m. To Dana's amazement, I dove in from Abner's Point exactly as Mark's digital watch turned 9:00:00 a.m.

The overcast skies and coastline fog of this ugly, gray day never allowed a ray of sunshine to peek through. I knew I would probably be dealing with this type of sensory deprivation in the Channel. In a long swim the sun makes a BIG difference since it warms the swimmer just a little bit but all the time. However, for this swim, the worse I had it, the better; this knowledge was only a small consolation.

Because of the clouds, the water remained a constant 61°F the entire day and the air was a comfortable 73°F and neither gave me any problems. Fortunately for my crew in the boat, it never rained.

Mark was superb in the boat, overseeing all my feedings and keeping track of the course. It was always such a comfort for me to see him, knowing that my needs and best interests were his priority.

Dana and David were wonderful. They wrote lots of messages on the grease board and made me laugh. Dana swam with me for an hour about three hours into the swim; the companionship was really nice. He kept up with me but remarked afterwards what amazing shape I was in, a sort of aquatic Energizer Bunny.

They displayed the "sprint" signs just as Terry had done the previous weekend and conveyed my stroke rate which ranged between 68 and 76 when I was in "forever pace" and shifted between 82 and 84 during the sprints.

Mark made sure I ate every half-hour, feasting mainly on a carbohydrate/protein drink mix, plus either tea, bananas, Fig Newtons, or animal crackers at every feeding. Dana and David did funny, amusing things with the animal crackers, nourishing my senses too. As time passed, the hotter liquids started to taste less hot, a sign that my inner core temperature was cooling down. However, I showed no other signs of being even mildly hypothermic.

I felt good for a long time. I was in a "hunkered down" state of mind, determined to make this long swim happen. Around six hours into it, I consciously increased my stroke rate to 76, eventually making the 'bellies' of my biceps tired. They were ready to stop, so what was I doing still relentlessly turning them over with no rest in sight? Soon thereafter, 'IT' hit, commonly known as 'The Wall'. Instead of being rendered immobile, I just returned to my previous slower pace. I still had no idea how much longer this swim was going to go on and amazingly, I did not ask. I was behaving very well.

Mark thought I looked cold. He sensed the slight ebb in my spirit even though I was still very cooperative and not complaining at all. In any case, my stroke rate remained constant at 74 with Pick Up increases to 82. At seven hours I let Mark know I was "a little tired."

Actually, my lower back had been killing me the whole time. During the previous week my sister, Gail, and her husband, Dave, had descended upon us with their two sons, Mark, age 2, and Brian, age 2 1/2 months. All week, 'Little Mark' kept us amused with his antics. I spent much of the week lifting and swinging him around and aggravating a compressed disc in my lower back. (When I was in England, Little Mark told everyone he knew that "Aunt Marcia went to 'Inglan' and she got alllll wet!")

I never let on how much my lower back hurt because my swimming was not affected, but I went so far as to stop doing flip turns during pool swims over the last few days. When this long swim began, I envisioned that everything would be OK if my entire lower half from the waist down could be removed, actually chopped off and hung up like a side of beef. I felt paralyzed.

My back hurt from stroke one. As planned from the week before, I took a Motrin beforehand and received another after six hours of swimming. I also got Liquid Tylenol every hour, which provided some relief. After about three hours of swimming, I realized that although the pain was constant, it was not getting any worse, and therefore not worth complaining about. It was just something I had to live with.

The course was the standard Abner's Point to Cook's and back, with the usual difficulty going in one direction, depending on which way the wind was blowing. That day the wind was calm: thank you, God! Sometime in the afternoon I was told that we would be pulling into the harbor just around the corner from Cook's which, of course, scared me to death even though the water was calmer than in Merriconeag Sound. The reason for this detour was easily understood by any kid: Josh had to call his mother. As an added bonus to the stop, anyone who wanted to use the bathroom (except me) could.

So I swam around Cook's Harbor for several minutes while all these details were taken care of. The water was cooler than in the Sound since the currents flowing under the Cribstone Bridge came in directly from the Atlantic.

Because Josh was playing in a hockey game that evening, Sandy Allen told her son to be home by 5 p.m. Accordingly, Mark, Dana and David decided to make this a seven-and-a half-hour day for me. As we approached Abner's Point for what I assumed would not be the last time of the day, Mark motioned to me to swim around the Point and into Mackerel Cove. After starting my aquatic day in the same spot seven-and-a half-hours earlier with a stroke rate of 72, I was now stroking 76 strokes a minute. I could not believe it was over, unless they were playing some trick on me. But it was—Hallelujah!

This swim sealed the deal for me. Over my 18 miles of swimming that day, despite all the distractions, several salt rashes, and very swollen lips and tongue, I knew I was ready. Shortly after we returned to our rented house to clean up, my brother, Bill arrived to visit. Within an hour of climbing out of the water I was seated at Cook's at a table overlooking the water from which I had just recently emerged. I was ready and I knew it!

Bill told me after my Channel swim that when he saw me in Maine he knew I would make it. Something about my confidence and determination.

Yea for Marcy!

On Monday July 4th, I found out that Marcy MacDonald had successfully swum the Channel on Thursday June 30th. I was thrilled for Marcy and knew if she could do it, so could I. However, the water temperature during her swim was 54°F which intimidated and scared me and made Marcy's performance so much more impressive. When I learned of her time; 10 hours and 33 minutes, I seriously started contemplating a fast swim too, if conditions were right and I didn't freeze my butt off in the process. My confidence kept waxing and waning even with all this extraordinary training behind me.

The Last Week: Alone and OK

I was alone during my final week in Maine. At first I was concerned that I would be lonely, but I wasn't at all. In addition to training up a storm, packing to go home, and reading *Midnight in the Garden of Good and Evil*, I wrote in a journal I had intended to keep, visualizing a successful swim. Before I knew it, Mark had arrived on Friday night for our final weekend together in Maine.

My last swim came on a fittingly beautiful day, Saturday, July 16th. In New York, before I left for Maine, I had been interviewed by a few magazines and newspapers. During this final swim, the local Portland news crew filmed my training and interviewed me afterwards, playing the footage that night on the 6 o'clock news. It was fun to watch.

When this swim was over, I was sad swimming into Mackerel Cove for the final time, but I knew I had done all this work for a reason: a successful English Channel swim was on the horizon. This was all part of the process and it was OK to feel temporarily saddened about leaving a place I had come to love, a place that played a big role in my Channel swim. The set of conditions I had trained in were optimal. It was just hard to say good-bye.

THE WEEK BEFORE ENGLAND

Maintaining my Acclimation

After returning to New York City from Maine on Sunday July 17th, I went back to work for one week. Every morning before going to the office I swam three miles in the John Jay Pool, one of my favorite outdoor pools in New York City, overlooking the East River. I had no problem maintaining the conditioning I had achieved in Maine but at 68°F to 70°F, the water was so warm that I was concerned about losing my acclimation to colder water. In the shower after my first swim, without any forethought,

I simply ignored the hot water faucet and continued with my cold showers. I felt as if I was right back in Merriconeag Sound.

During the week I packed my equipment and clothes. I was a coiled spring ready to let go. All the preparation was coming to a head.

EIGHT

To England

THE NARROWEST PART OF THE ENGLISH Channel, from Dover, England to Cap Gris Nez, France, is known as the Strait of Dover. The volume of water being pushed through this 23 mile stretch is affected by the tides—spring or neap—which in turn are affected by the phases of the moon.

During a spring tide when the moon is either full or new, the difference between high and low water in the English Channel is often 18 to 20 feet, approximately three to six feet more than during the neap tides, when the moon is at quarters. Consequently, more water flows through the Strait of Dover during a spring tide than during a neap, thus creating a greater amount of water to push a swimmer around. Because of this, the six to nine day periods of neap tides are slightly more favorable for swimmers, although they may swim on any tide they want. Good weather is more important. My neap tide window was July 29th to August 6th.

Taking Off, Finally

An American Airlines flight leaves John F. Kennedy Airport in New York City for Heathrow Airport in London at 9 a.m. every day. On Saturday July 23rd, I was on this flight. As the plane took off over Jamaica Bay and headed east, I could see Rockaway below. Today was the day I had thought about when I swam there and saw planes taking off, bound for Europe. I knew some day I would be on one of those planes and this day had finally arrived.

If I had had a map, I would have been able to follow the coastline better, but I soon realized we were flying over Martha's Vineyard and Nantucket, then over Maine and Nova Scotia, and finally out over the Atlantic Ocean. I thought about all the people in Maine who had helped me and wondered what they were doing at the moment.

The plane flew into the sunset and landed at 9 p.m. at Heathrow Airport. The airport seemed deserted. Going through customs and picking up the luggage happened without a hitch. When the customs officer asked why I was in England, I proudly told him, "I'm here to swim the Channel." He smiled and wished me good luck.

I felt a sense of mission. By crossing the Atlantic I was finally, totally, and even geographically, committed. When I left the European continent, I would have either successfully swum the English Channel, or at the very least, given it my best shot.

Once I emerged into the warm and muggy London night, I continued to feel this sense of mission. I did not feel the relaxation that comes with being on vacation. That would come later.

Checking In

From the Heathrow rental car office at 10:30 p.m., I called Audrey and Bill Hamblin, the proprietors of Victoria Guest House in Dover, to let them know that the plane had arrived safely and I would be on my way momentarily. Bill promised to wait up. I had received high recommendations for Victoria Guest House as an ideal spot for Channel swimmers in several ways; most importantly because Audrey and Bill seem to understand the needs of Channel swimmers.

There are several hotels and guest houses in Dover and Folkestone listed in the Channel Information Pack. All of them provide superb accommodations and care for Channel swimmers. A recommendation from a previous swimmer is a great way to determine where to stay.

I also called Mark, an ocean away. The only reason we had been physically separated most of the summer was because of my desire to conquer the Channel. I felt a great deal of responsibility for having everything work out. I missed him all the time and it would have been comforting if we had been together this night in this unfamiliar, dark land. I didn't know it at the time, but there would be many other things I would have to do by myself during the next week and I was on my own in a big way. It was time to sink or swim.

Mark and Terry were scheduled to arrive at Heathrow on Wednesday morning July 27th. There were not many things for them to do until the actual swim. My mother and two of her friends would be coming on the same flight. They planned to provide enthusiastic ground support during my swim.

The road to Dover, the A20, winds along the English Channel for several miles. Driving on this road at night, the Channel looked pitch black. I knew it was out there, over those cliffs, but it was out of sight. For prospective Channel swimmers, this road seems to tease and taunt.

Victoria Guest House

It was weird to be arriving in Dover, no less finding the Victoria Guest House. After three years of actively planning this trip, I was actually here. Dover was more cosmopolitan than I had anticipated and I quickly discovered that it has most of the necessary amenities for Channel swimmers; I could have left a full suitcase or two at home.

The Victoria Guest House (VGH) lies a few hundred meters from the town's center, Market Square. It is part of a row of well-maintained, four-story houses of typical English architecture. Colorful flowers dot all the window boxes. As I pulled up the sloping street at 2 a.m., the door of VGH opened and I was immediately greeted by Bill Hamblin.

Bill and his wife, Audrey, run Victoria Guest House. Bill put me at ease right away and told me how much they enjoy hosting their Channel swimmers; most recently, Marcy. He helped me with the bags and led me up the narrow staircase to my room on the third floor. If I was up for it, breakfast would be served between 7 and 10 a.m. I sensed I would be comfortable and well cared for here, one less thing to worry about.

When I got into bed, it was only 9 p.m. New York time. I was not particularly tired but I knew tomorrow I would attempt to adjust to the five-hour time difference in one day. By not taking a desperately desired nap on Sunday afternoon, and forcing myself to stay up until bedtime, by Monday morning I had acclimated to English time the hard way.

Meeting Many New Friends

When my alarm went off at 7 a.m. Sunday morning, I ached momentarily, but got myself together and proceeded down to breakfast. It was here that I met Audrey Hamblin. Since so many Channel swimmers have stayed with them, Audrey and Bill pride themselves on their success with swimmers. Up to that point, all the swimmers who had stayed with them had succeeded with their Channel swims. They know what prepared swimmers look like, physically and mentally. Audrey said she could always see it "in the eyes." I would know what she meant in five days.

Audrey and Bill also know how to feed Channel swimmers. Breakfast consisted of a parade of food: cereal, eggs, ham, juice, toast, butter, and jam. We were reminded cheerfully and continuously by our two hosts that we "had to keep our strength up." It was a caloric and cholesterol extravaganza every morning.

It was also at this breakfast that I met Nora Toledano Cadena, a Mexican woman with an infectious smile. She was attempting her second Two Way Channel Swim; swimming over to France and back to England without stopping. She had done a One Way in 1992.

Nora and I quickly became good friends. Bill had told me when I made my reservations in March that Nora would be staying with them at the same time. Nora and I soon figured out that we had done similar types of work to get to where we were and an innate understanding developed. I was inspired by Nora, knowing that she put even more time and energy into her training than I did.

Nora is a seasoned veteran of the English Channel. As she stepped out of the water after her Channel swim in 1992, she thought then and there she could do a Two Way. On June 30, 1994, she had set a Mexican record of 9:40 during the first leg of her initial Two Way attempt. (She and Marcy both did their swims at the same time.) On the return leg, as a result of the bone-chilling 54°F water, she decided to end this Two Way attempt after 15 hours and chose to wait and try again a few weeks later. In the interim, she trained every day in the harbor and also did a Channel relay with five other swimmers.

She taught me the ropes, both in and out of the water, and answered my last minute questions, such as "What type of bathing cap should I wear?" since I was still not sure.

She gave me the soft silicone orange one I eventually wore during my swim, with the Channel Swimming logo printed on it. Also, she answered my anxious, continual inquiries of, "Do I have everything I need?" and "Am I prepared?"

Nora was amazed at my preparation. Assurance seems to be one of those basic human needs. I just wanted <u>the</u>

affirming statement: "Yes, Marcia. You have done absolutely everything you need to do for this and everything will work out just fine," and I have yet to receive (or give) it.

Nora's assurance was probably the closest I came to feeling I would be all right if I just kept moving forward. With the English Channel, there are no guarantees.

When Nora successfully completed her Two Way swim the week after my swim, I was honored to be one of her crew members and her swimming pacer. Her swim was truly amazing. On August 6th, 1994, after swimming for 23 hours, 38 minutes, Nora became the sixth woman in history to swim a Two Way of the English Channel, the 20th person ever, and the first Latin American woman.

Arriving at Dover Harbour

After breakfast on that first morning, Nora and I went down to Dover Harbour together. I had only a vague idea of what to expect, based on pictures I had seen in Channel literature. Being with Nora allowed me to get acquainted quickly with the Harbour. It was very nice of her to take me under her wing but I noticed this type of immediate camaraderie among Channel swimmers.

Nora introduced me to about 15 other Channel swimmers, some of whom had already swum and others who were Channel Wannabes like me. It was exciting to be a part of this Channel history-in-the-making yet a vague underlying tension existed, knowing that some of us would be successful and some would not.

I met Alison Streeter and found her to be an extremely down-to-earth person. I liked her right away and respected her straight-forward, no-nonsense approach. She told me that England was having its best summer weather in years. When I met her, she had swum the Channel 24 times and was chasing the overall record of 31 crossings. On September 3, 1995, Alison broke this record with her 32nd crossing, hence becoming, in her words, "Monarch of the Channel." As of July 2007, she has 43 individual crossings to her credit and was inducted into the International Swimming Hall of Fame in May 2006.

I also met Alison's mother, Freda. She is intricately involved in Alison's swimming and is an experienced presence on the beach. Her assistance to swimmers with advice, equipment, and training ideas is legendary.

I introduced myself to Freda, "Hi, I'm Marcia from the United States."

Freda told me she had heard of me and asked, "When do you swim?"

"On Friday, with Mike Oram."

Even before I arrived in England, I had it set in my mind that I was going to swim the English Channel on July 29th or later, but now telling pros like Freda a specific date made the whole thing very real.

I was rational and tidy about what was going to happen between the time I arrived in Dover and my Channel swim. It would be a regular week for me including, "and on Friday, I'll swim the English Channel."

My plans for the week worked out to be:

Sunday July 24th: 2-hour swim, no nap (no matter how tired), visit Langdon Cliffs.

Monday July 25th: 2 1/2 hour swim, collect last minute equipment, optional sightsee to Museum, call Mike Oram.

Tuesday July 26th: 1 1/2 hour swim, optional sightsee to Castle.

Wednesday July 27th: Pick up Mark and Terry at the Airport, 1 hour swim.

Thursday July 28th: 30 minute swim, pack bags, crew meeting, confirm with Mike.

Friday July 29th: Swim the English Channel.

Saturday & Sunday July 30th and 31st: Recover, sightsee, Celebrate! Celebrate!

But the actual situation could be completely different and I knew it. Sometimes weeks go by without any swimmable days, resulting in swimmers having to wait around anxiously and worry, among other things, about their training. How much swimming was enough to maintain a good feel for the water and proper conditioning, but not too much to be tired for a Channel attempt? I was *extremely* lucky to have good weather on the first day of my neap tides and I nailed my final training as a result. In fact, the weather in Europe that summer turned out to be unusually good, resulting in 38 successful solo crossings out of approximately 64 attempts, an extraordinary 60% success rate. Typically, in recent times, only about 30 to 40% of attempts are successful.

Fred & Molly, the Quiet Observers

Fred Hammond was on the beach that Sunday, as he is almost every single day of the year. He has been watching Channel swimmers train in Dover Harbour for 40 years and has seen it all. I affectionately dubbed him "The Mayor of Dover Harbour." He and his friend, Molly, kept an accurate eye on almost every swimmer in the water and knew where every one was most of the time. This is quite a feat, especially when there could be 20-odd swimmers in the Harbour at once. Fred also makes time predictions which he will reveal only after a swimmer makes a successful crossing. He told me the day after my swim, based on what he saw of my conditioning and acclimation that he thought I could do it in about 10 hours.

First Encounters

Five days before my planned swim, I had my first actual physical contact with the Channel. I simply, calmly, and confidently thought, "I'm going to make it," as I waded into Dover Harbour. Even though there were lots of things going on out of my control that made me feel uneasy, I had this inner feeling that in a bathing suit, swimming next to a boat, I could swim to the other side. As I waded further in, the water temperature felt fine. It was actually warmer than the water in Maine. All the planning, all the preparation, and now, it was really happening!

On that first day, Nora and I swam for two hours in the Harbour, going "Wall to Wall." Dover Harbour is larger but calmer than I expected and shaped like a wide, flattened U. Looking at it from land, the left (east) side of the U is where the ferries and gigantic container ships dock at enormous steel piers. The right (west) side is Admiralty Pier, the spot from which Matthew Webb started his Channel swim. On the other side of this pier is the spot where the Hovercraft used to land. The Hovercraft, a giant hydro-ferry, makes cross-Channel passages in about 60 minutes. The constant sound of a far-off rumble can be heard all over Dover when the Hovercraft is approaching shore and docking.

Aerial view of Dover Harbour. The dock for the Hovercraft is in the center of the photo. Admiralty Pier ends at the middle right.

Past the Hovercraft, further over to the west, are the Western Docks where small crafts tie up, including some of the Channel pilot boats.

The bottom part of the U is the swimming beach. To the middle left of this bottom part is where Channel swimmers and their merry bands hang out. Across the top of the U is a breakwater that keeps the Harbour waters fairly calm. Nora taught me that the typical swim course of about 1,500 meters (about 1 mile) is to swim from one side of the U to the other, better known as "Wall to Wall." (Since 1994, the eastern piers have been extended slightly into the swimming area of the Harbour, thus shortening the swim course to about 1,300 meters (about 0.8 miles).

A round trip for us, from the beach, to the east side, over to the west side, and back to the beach was about an hour—perfect timing for feedings. Usually someone among the Channel watchers would see us approaching and bring our feeding bottles to us in the water. It was cool to think that these people liked us and helped us simply because we were aspiring Channel swimmers.

During the last part of our Sunday swim, a speedy swimmer joined us. Since the Harbour water is chalky, I could not tell if it was a man or a woman; he or she was wearing only bathing trunks. When we arrived back at the beach, Nora introduced me to this mysterious, happy, vivacious swimmer: Tammy Van Wisse, a 26-year-old Australian woman. She had a gorgeous tan and did not appear bulked up to me.

On Monday I found out that during the previous week Tammy and her 21-year-old brother, John, had become the first brother-sister duo to swim the Channel at the same time. John finished in 8 hours, 17 minutes; Tammy was right behind him in 8 hours, 33 minutes. The previous year Tammy had won the Rolex watch which is awarded to the person with the fastest swim of the year. For her 1993 effort of 8 hours, 35 minutes, she received the watch and it was given to her on Monday. She politely showed it to all of us on the beach. I was impressed with Tammy and John for their accomplishments. They helped me see that "Yes, this really is do-able."

Another Australian who was in Dover at the same time was 14-year-old Kelly Dixon. She became the youngest Australian to swim the Channel, swimming two days after me, in 9 hours 38 minutes. Mike Oram said that every year there is "one perfect swimming day" and Kelly happened to get it in 1994. During practice swims in Dover Harbour Kelly exhibited great bravado and would go right up and touch the steep, steel, slimy dock walls. I was never that brave and always turned around about ten meters from the walls. Kelly yelled at Nora and me as we swam together, chiding in her local accent, "You're not supposed to swim together!" (Her father had told her this. I completely disagreed.)

We ignored her because of her young age and our own compatibility. (Nora sarcastically referred to her as "Coach.") I found that in Dover Harbour, along with every other swimming hole in the world, it was OK to swim with other swimmers just as long as I was getting in the training I wanted to and liked who I was swimming with.

Another American swimmer I met was Laura Burtch from San Francisco. She had been on a successful relay swim in 1992 but did not make it as a solo swimmer in 1993. She told me that during her attempted solo she spent an hour swimming through a shoal of jellyfish and was seriously stung which caused a nauseous reaction. Consequently, she could not keep food down and had to abort her swim about six hours into it. (No one else who swam the Channel that day even saw a jellyfish; they are completely random.) Her story was very disconcerting to hear the day before I swam; actually, it totally freaked me out. Fortunately she made a successful 11 hour, 45 minute swim on Saturday July 30th.

Confidence Boosters!

I loved swimming with Nora and we got together almost every day. We were very similar in abilities and it gave me a lot of confidence to know that yes, in fact, I could do this. Meeting all of these swimmers was the first time in three years that I truly knew I had the endurance it takes to swim the English Channel. I realized I was in just as good shape as most of the others, especially the ones who were doing fast times, and I believed I would be successful.

After swimming in the 64/65°F water of the Harbour, I would towel off and not feel cold. Back at Victoria Guest House I would take a cold shower, letting myself warm up naturally. From the third day on in the Harbour I wore my workout bikini because the water temperature felt so comfortable. Things were coming together.

Meeting people from different countries helped me to learn to make measurement conversions in a hurry, such as temperature and distance. Most of the rest of the world measures distance in kilometers and temperature in Celsius degrees. I learned to talk in this new "language" so I could quickly make sense of the numbers that were discussed, most importantly, mastering the conversions of Fahrenheit and Celsius degrees between 55° and 65° Fahrenheit.

Indian Children

There were three 12-year-old Indian children in Dover that summer attempting to swim the Channel. Fred predicted that the 12-year-old Indian boy who swam on the same day I did would finish in about 12 hours. Actually, Rihen Mehta finished in 11 hours, 33 minutes. Seeing Rihen train in the Harbour, I knew he had the mental attitude and body fat to make it across. It just concerned me that he was attempting such a major undertaking at such a young age. The day after Rihen made his swim, everyone in the Channel community was invited to an elaborate Indian-style reception in his honor at the Grand Hotel in Folkestone, a new cultural experience for most of us, especially due to the fact that it lacked adult-style beverages. After the two other 12-year-old Indian children also made successful swims, the minimum age requirement was changed to 16 years, a decision implicitly understood by most of us in the Channel swimming world.

Bob West: Story Teller

Through Fred Hammond I met Bob West, an American from San Diego, who was in Dover with Cerise Calvin, another Channel swimmer from the United States. Bob assured me that I would be OK since I looked good while training in the Harbour and had the necessary body fat. He and Fred had a wonderful time recounting stories of failed attempts, such as the Egyptian who decided he would take a nap four hours into his swim, only to be angrily awoken by a huge oar from his escort boat slapping the water right next to his head. Bob and Fred both reassured me, "Women do fine. It's the men who have all the psycho stories." I secretly hoped so.

There were some people on the beach whom I did not believe were going to be successful. With the exception of the Indian children, none of them were successful that summer. One swimmer seemed to lack the confidence, and had difficulty looking anyone in the eye. Another explained that she was back this year because: "Last year after 14 hours, I was still six miles off the coast of France and was told I would be in the water another eight hours." This swimmer was about 40 pounds overweight. It was obvious that too much body fat does not help in getting one across the Channel.

All week the weather forecast for Friday continued to be good. I collected last minute equipment and familiarized myself with Dover. I also did a lot of "futzing around," simply killing time by arranging and re-arranging my stuff, looking busy when, in fact, I was just very anxious. The town turned out to be larger than I expected and it has a lovely pedestrian mall. I did a little sightseeing to Langdon Cliffs, the Dover Museum, and Dover Castle.

Dover Castle sits atop the White Cliffs, overlooking the Channel, and is visible from almost everywhere in Dover. It was built around the 12th century and has successfully held off all invaders. The Channel waters probably have something to do with this record too. The castle constitutes the left side of the CSA emblem, complemented on the right side by the Cap Gris Nez Lighthouse. Freda Streeter says she can always tell which way the wind is blowing in the middle of the Channel from the direction that the flag is blowing on top of the Castle.

When I visited the Castle on Tuesday, France was obscured by the Channel haze. Of course I tried to look across, thinking that it was a long way to swim but, thanks to the weather, I could not see the opposite coast. By the time Mark arrived on Wednesday, the view to France was vaguely clear. It was almost as if the Channel

Gods were deciding when and what they wanted me to see.

People in Dover do not consider swimming the English Channel a big deal since Channel swimmers descend upon the town every summer, hence there is minimal local press coverage. Although the concept of swimming the Channel seems to be a major event in the United States, the press coverage is nominal in America as well.

I phoned Mark on Sunday, Monday, and Tuesday from Market Square in downtown Dover. From there Mark could hear the ever-present squawking seagulls. Mainly the conversations were reassuring chit-chats. It was a big, huge, gigantic relief to see him walk out of customs at Heathrow on Wednesday morning, July 27th. Once Mark and Terry arrived all the components for a successful swim were in place.

Crew Knowledge

For the start all I needed to find were my goggles and bathing cap but it was very important for Mark and Terry to know where all the equipment was packed. After breakfast Mark and Terry sent me down to the Harbour so they could pack the equipment bags in peace. *(Sitting on the bed making suggestions to them about how to pack was not winning me any friends.)* When I returned the bags were organized, packed and labeled. Some of the labels included a category, such as *Post-Swim I & II, Secondary Foods, and FDS (Food Delivery System).* This new acronym made me laugh, especially since Mark & Terry took themselves so seriously.

Mark and Terry had designed an innovative feeding pole which swung with gravity. The "Food Delivery System," soon to become known only as the "FDS," was constructed from a 6" x 9" wire basket that was connected with duct tape to the end of a broom handle. To keep three 16-ounce cups upright for me, Mark and Terry stretched a piece of wire lengthwise down the middle of the basket which divided the basket in half. The cup half of the basket was then divided by wire into three equal sections, one for each cup, while the other half of the basket remained empty.

Confirmations

While I was swimming that morning, Mike Oram called the guest house to find out if I was ready for my swim the next day. Mark told him I was ready. Mike asked that we meet him at the Western Docks at 3 a.m. He also wanted me to call him at 7 p.m. that evening for a final confirmation. Everything was handled calmly: my Channel swim was going to happen on Friday, July 29th. I was extremely fortunate that everything went smoothly.

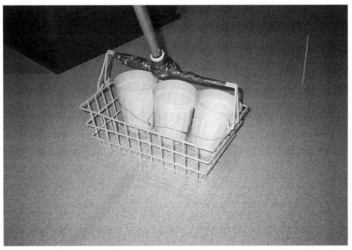

The FDS (Food Delivery System).

We did a practice drive to the Western Docks on Thursday afternoon. Mike's dock was a little difficult to locate and we did not need any additional confusion at 3 a.m. My mother was planning to watch my start so she did a practice drive to Shakespeare Beach.

During our final crew meeting I told Mark and Terry that I thought I could swim the Channel in nine to ten hours if weather conditions allowed. By stating this goal my crew could calculate the type of pace that I would have to establish early on then maintain in order to achieve such a result.

We decided that Mark would videotape as much of the actual swim as possible. We added a pre-swim interview before dinner and optimistically planned a celebratory post-swim conversation as well. In the pre-swim interview, I appear meek and scared but an underlying focus and confidence exists. I felt an invisible weight perched on my shoulder as I described my preparation for this "enormous undertaking."

At one point in the pre-swim interview I said, "I know the hard part is behind me."

Mark asks, "So you feel that in your mind?"

I shot back, "I *know* that!"

I so deeply wished for this upcoming Channel swim to go well.

I got into bed around 7:30 p.m. Thursday night and set the alarm for 2 a.m. on Friday July 29th: *The Day.* Trying to fall asleep, I kept vacillating between amazement and fright, thinking, "I'm going to be swimming the English Channel in a couple of hours." Forget about sleeping the night before a big event.

Nora came in around 8 p.m. to wish me good luck and to tell me I would be OK. I thought a lot about the advice she had given me earlier in the week, "The water along the coast is rough but out in the middle its smoother, so get going! Zoom!"

As Nora left, she gave me the two thumbs up sign. I would see this image of her many, many times in the next 24 hours.

Mark came to bed around 10 p.m. but neither of us could get to sleep. It's always like that: on nights you have to get to sleep, no way. Finally, around midnight, I fell into a fitful slumber.

THE DAY

The alarm sounded at 2 a.m. It was time—my time. After stretching and applying one coat of suntan lotion to soak in, I ate a quick bowl of cream of rice. Terry ate two bowls of Sugar Pops (he would regret both later), and Mark had his usual nothing. The bags were ready to go, we packed the car, and off we went.

This all seemed to be happening in a nervous dream. Who was I to be getting up in the middle of the night, to do something as far-fetched as swimming in cold, dark water from one foreign country to another? How had I managed to finagle Mark and Terry into this scene as well? With these and other silent questions circulating, the conversation in the car was limited. A calm tension existed; we all wondered what the day's outcome would be, knowing that the English Channel is a finicky beast even when at its best.

3 AM

We arrived at the Western boat dock and met Mike Oram, the boat pilot, and his son and first mate, Lance, for the first time. They were already prepping the *Aegean Blue*. This 33-foot boat seemed to be just the right size to swim alongside and from which to receive feedings. It had state-of-art navigational equipment, including a Global Positioning

System, which enabled Mike to plot our exact course and determine water currents. There was a stove and, for the weary, a bunk to sleep in down below. Overall, it was (and is) an excellent vessel for Channel swimmers. Mike Oram claims a success rate of 80 to 90% with Channel swimmers. He wants each and every one of them to make it. If you want to get out, he asks that you say three times in a row, **"I am a complete failure."** He claims that no one has ever gotten through that statement three times!

All of the Channel Pilots are excellent and have superb equipment for Channel swimmers, similar to that found on the Aegean Blue. There are several pilots from which to choose. All of them care about each and every one of their swimmers. Most are based either in Dover or Folkestone.

ABOUT 3:20 AM

Everything was still and quiet. I felt very nervous as we loaded the boat because I knew I was going to be swimming in the dark soon, and that scared me. In New York it was 10 p.m. and everyone back home was probably heading for bed. In these pre-internet days, no one at home knew I was boarding the boat for my Channel swim. I thought about my Dad and my siblings and sent them mental messages:

"While you are sleeping tonight, I'll be swimming the Channel."

An official observer for each swimmer is designated a day or two before an attempt is made. My observer, Norman Trusty, had been observing Channel swimmers for years. With three successful solo swims of his own, he was a seasoned pro. (He also turned out to be one of Nora's observers so I was able to talk with him during her swim.)

Aegean Blue pulled away from the dock and headed for the Dover Harbor Breakwater. Among those on board were Mike Oram, Lance Oram, Norman Trusty, Mark Green, Terry Tyner, and me. But I would be leaving soon. Except for occasional nervous chit-chat, it was quiet. The swells going through the Breakwater were rough and we were tossed around a lot. Suddenly I silently doubted that I could swim this Channel because how on earth was I going to swim in water that was this rough and very possibly rougher?! Very soon I was going to find out what I was made of. THIS WAS FOR REAL AND IT WAS HAPPENING RIGHT NOW.

The boat headed west towards Shakespeare Beach but did not get any closer to the shore. When we were almost past it, I frantically asked Mike where we were going because my mother and her two friends were waiting there for the start. I had no idea there were any other starting points, and I had always thought I would start from "Shaky."

He explained, "We're going from Abbot Cliff right next to the Channel Tunnel."

I had never heard of it.

"It's a small, new private beach cleared two years ago by the Tunnel Works, the builders of the Channel Tunnel. From what you've told me, you're a fairly quick swimmer. If you want to go to Shakespeare, you'll add an hour to your time because you won't catch the high tide as quickly which will push you east faster."

I started my swim from Abbot Cliff.

Mike had determined my starting time and place based on several factors: my predicted swimming pace after a few hours combined with the tide schedules on that specific day and a planned finish at Cap Gris Nez. Using these elements, he always figures a swim "backwards" to optimize the swimmer's ability. Swimmers with Mike Oram start from all over either coast (depending on the direction of their swim) at all hours of the day and night.

As *Aegean Blue* headed towards Abbot Cliff, I glanced towards France and said, "Oh look, you can see the lights on the French coast." Lance happened to be listening and calmly replied, "Oh no. Those are ships in the shipping lanes and we're heading right towards them."

Later I would think of these ships as friends but at that moment I wanted to get sick.

ABOUT 3:55 AM

It was time to grease up. This is a messy job and has to be done at the last possible moment because once you are greased up you have to stand around as is; wrapping a towel around yourself would create a gigantic mess. Mark put on heavy rubber gloves and applied a second coat of suntan lotion to me. He then opened the container of "grease" (one part lanolin and three parts Vaseline) that we had mixed, and started slathering me with a few pounds of it. He put grease all over my back, legs, and armpits; the areas from which I lost the most heat. He also put it just under my bathing suit line and on my neck to prevent chafing. I did not want grease on my hands, feet, or arms, as that would minimize my feel for the water. I also have a tendency to brush my goggles with my biceps on the recovery portion of my arm stroke, so I did not want to risk smearing my goggles. Being greased up always reminds me of what a horse must feel like when it is being shod. You simply have to stand there and take it while someone else gets rather personal with you.

Mike wanted to know why the grease was not white and teased us, "Ah, secret American grease."

The reason our grease was not white was because I had brought anhydrous lanolin with me from the United States. The Channel grease mixture available from Boots Chemist in Dover is white because it contains hydrous lanolin. (Boots is a drugstore chain in the UK.) The only difference between the two types is color. If I had known I would have ordered grease from Boots when I arrived in Dover instead of carrying several pounds of the stuff over the Atlantic.

True to my expectations, most of the grease disappeared within the first two hours. Only a very thin layer made it to France. But that was all right; like body fat, grease doesn't get you across the English Channel.

The boat was rocking in the swells as Mark greased me up. I held on to Terry's shoulders so I would not fall. I was shaking and Terry realized my serious anxiety. He did not try to joke around. Instead he just calmly told me, "You're ready for this. You've worked hard. You're going to do well."

What he said was what I needed to hear.

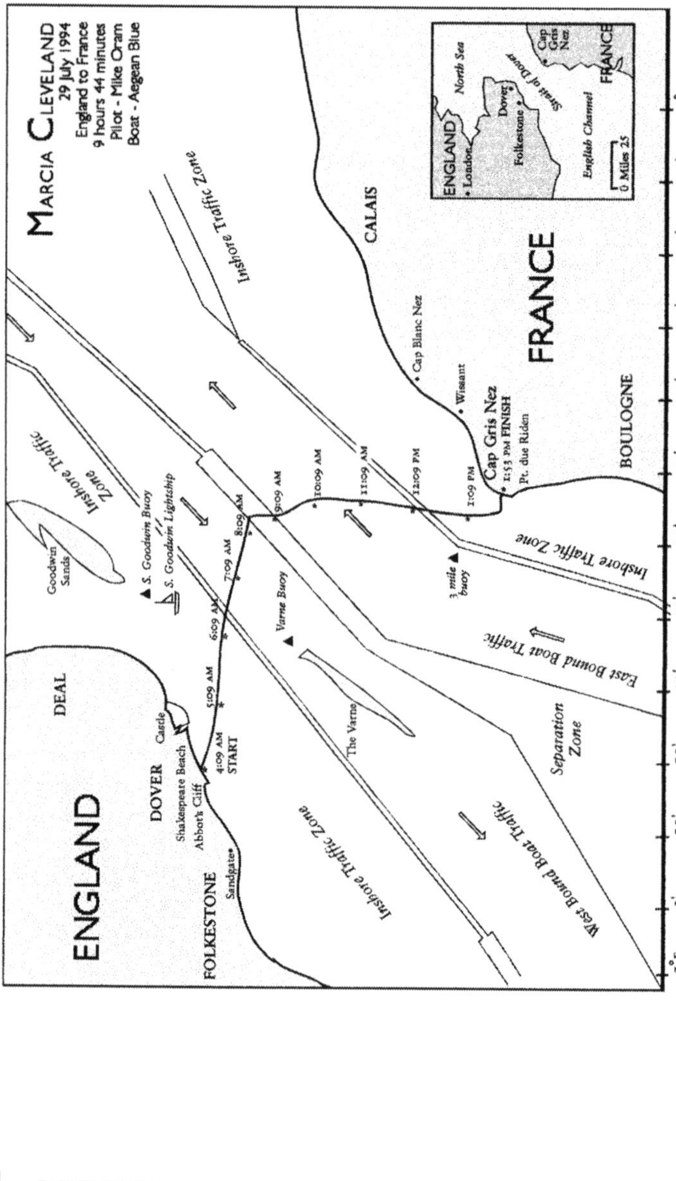

Marcia Cleveland
29 July 1994
England to France
9 hours 44 minutes
Pilot - Mike Oram
Boat - Aegean Blue
ENGLAND
FOLKESTONE
Sandgate
Abbot's Cliff
Shakespeare Beach
DOVER
Castle
DEAL
4:09 AM
START
5:09 AM
6:09 AM
7:09 AM
8:09 AM
9:09 AM
10:09 AM
11:09 AM
12:09 PM
1:09 PM
1:53 PM FINISH
Goodwin Sands
S. Goodwin Buoy
S. Goodwin Lightship
Varne Buoy
The Varne
Inshore Traffic Zone
Inshore Traffic Zone
Inshore Traffic Zone
Inshore Traffic Zone
West Bound Boat Traffic
East Bound Boat Traffic
Separation Zone
3 mile buoy
FRANCE
CALAIS
Cap Blanc Nez
Wissant
Cap Gris Nez
Pt. due Riden
BOULOGNE
ENGLAND
London
Dover
Folkestone
North Sea
Strait of Dover
Cap Gris Nez
English Channel
FRANCE
0 Miles 25
1° E
5'
10'
15'
20'
25'
30'
35'
40'
45'
50'
55'
2° E

NINE

Swimming the English Channel

4 AM: THE START

The rules of the start and finish of a Channel swim are clearly stated by the associations:

> "For a swim to be officially recognised, the swimmer must walk into the sea from the shore of departure, swim across the English Channel (i) to finish on dry land, or (ii) to touch steep cliffs, of the opposite coast with no seawater beyond." (Rule 10C, Channel Swimming & Piloting Federation; Rule b, CSA.)

Because I was required to start from dry land I had to swim from the boat to the shore, a distance of about 20 yards. At a few minutes after 4 a.m. it was time to begin my swim of the English Channel. There was nothing ceremonious about my start. Mike pinned a light stick to the back of my suit, pointed towards the dark shore, and said, "The beach is that way."

I could barely make out a narrow pile of stones backed by a dark cliff. I kicked off my shoes, kissed Mark goodbye, and walked to the back of the boat. I felt as if I was about to walk the plank and the sharks were hungry below. *(Fortunately there are no sharks in the English Channel—it's too cold.)* The thing I was most aware of was that I was shaking from fear.

Was this really happening? I heard Mike say matter-of-factly, "OK. Let's go."

It was the moment of truth. I stepped onto the backboard of the *Aegean Blue.* The water washed over my feet and, to my joyful astonishment, the 58°F water felt fine. I hesitated for a second, took a deep breath, and jumped into the pitch black water.

In an instant I was 10 yards from both the boat and the beach. I put a foot down to feel for the bottom: Nothing. It was not there. Five more yards, still nothing. Only at the shoreline did I finally feel the sharp slope of the bottom as I clawed my way up the cold, pebbled beach below Abbot Cliff.

The orange glow of the lightstick pinned to the back of my suit made me visible to everyone on the boat. My observer, Norman Trusty, could see that I had gotten out of the water and was now ready to begin my journey to France.

An American Start

At 4:09 a.m., I waded from England's dry land back into the water for the start of my swim. My predominant thought at the time was, "It's going to be a long time until I touch land again."

It escaped me that I had inadvertently smeared both my hands with grease. As I had jumped off the boat, unconsciously I had put my hands on my greased-up thighs. At the start of my swim, I pressed my palms against my goggles to secure them, thus transferring the grease. All I could make out now through this "Crisco view" was light and darkness, and there was plenty of the latter.

I suddenly remembered other things I had forgotten to do. There I was: twenty-five yards into the start of my Channel swim, already disoriented by grease and darkness, yelling to Mark, "I just smeared my goggles and need new ones *right now*, and I forgot to put drops in my ears, and I forgot to put Vaseline on my lips."

Because he had packed the bags, Mark instantly found everything I needed and put these items in the feeding basket. He lowered it over the side of the boat as Mike blew the air horn to alert me. I ripped off my smeared goggles, threw them into the basket, and grabbed the new goggles by the strap. Careful not to touch the lenses, I quickly put the new pair on, grabbed the ear drops that Mark had put in a paper cup and squirted a few drops in each ear. Mark had put Vaseline inside the rim of another cup so I took that cup in my mouth, licked the rim, let it drop into the water, and finally, grabbed the paper towel from the basket and wiped most of the grease off my hands. This entire pit stop only took about 30 seconds but it was not one of the more organized starts of a Channel swim. I can only imagine what Mike Oram must have been thinking about spending this possibly very long day with "The Americans."

I finally got my act together.

The water got deep quickly and the current picked up right away. My arms turned over fast, fueled by nervous energy. I felt strong. The slight wind created a two-foot chop, a condition we would have all day. Mike aimed a spotlight on me as I swam within 10 feet of the boat. I was very conscious that every stroke was taking me further away from land. So this is what swimming the English Channel was like: totally freaky, totally frantic, very scary, and incredibly exciting.

Within minutes I was even with the Dover Harbour Breakwater and heading into the wide-open English Channel. Goodbye security. I forced myself to continue and not stop to tell the crew how scared I was. Then I recalled what Marcy had said, *"Every stroke is taking you one stroke closer to France."*

I knew I had to keep on taking one more stroke again and again, even as scared as I was. To try and fail after giving it my best effort would be no disgrace, but I had not given it my best effort yet.

Everything that I planned to think about went out the window. I forgot about stroke mechanics and swam on sheer instinct. Never in my wildest dreams did I realize or anticipate the mettle it would take at the beginning. All the organization and preparation was of little matter if I could not deal with the psychological stresses here and now. I had the ability to swim the distance but, at this moment, I was not sure if I had the grit. Would I become one more of Fred and Bob's "psycho stories"? I had to actively think about summoning courage from within during those first few moments, and learning the first of many lessons that the English Channel would teach me that day. Those first two hours were my most challenging part of the swim.

Those familiar with Channel swimming say that if you can see across the Channel, from England to France, it's too windy to swim. Therefore most swims start with the swimmer heading out into obscurity, swimming alongside the escort boat.

When I started my swim it was pitch black and that spooked me. Not only could I not see my final destination, I had no idea of what kind of marine life and man-made objects I might encounter en route. I was fearful of running into jellyfish, especially after talking with Laura Burtch (and being sure those jellies were now just waiting for me!) Swimming in the dark away from land is one of the scariest things I had ever done, and I was now wishing I had practiced this beforehand. But I had not and I had to deal with it now, or fail.

As I got through it, I reminded myself of the many Channel swimmers who had done this before. This was all part of the process of being successful. But I will never allow myself to forget the fear and how difficult it was to overcome. I only relaxed when daylight came two hours later.

Starting out, Mike prefers to have swimmers on the port (left) side so he can see them directly from the wheelhouse as he steers. After an hour Mike switched me over to the starboard (right) side so the boat would act as a slight barrier to the choppy water of the westbound high tide. Although Mike was not able see me as well on the starboard side, we quickly adapted to each other's styles. It didn't matter to me which side of the boat I swam on, but I preferred to swim 10 to 15 feet from the side of the boat, near the back area where Mark and Terry were sitting. It was easier for me to communicate from this position so, for the most part, Mike kept the boat there.

Calming Mantras in the Beginning

During this time the song *I Can See Clearly Now The Rain is Gone* came into my head. I have no idea when or where I last heard it but I sang it over and over again and it helped to calm me down.

"I can see clearly now the rain is gone…"
(It was dark and cloudy at the time.)
"I can see all obstacles in my way…"
(I could see only the glaring bright light spotting me from the boat. I couldn't see a thing in the water.)
"Gone are those dark clouds that had me blind…"
(They were all around, keeping me "blind.")

"…It's gonna be a bright, bright sunshiny day."

(Although I had no idea at the time, this turned out to be true.)

I also thought about a lot of the people who had helped me get to this point. They believed in me and wanted me to make it; I didn't want to let them down. I knew I could make this happen, to make this all worthwhile. To give myself courage and strength, I started to say over and over to myself *"Yes, You Can; Yes, You Can; Yes, You Can."*

A favorite inspirational saying also came to mind:

Ask not for victory alone, ask for courage. For if you can endure, you bring honor to yourself. Even more, you bring honor to us all.

On board, Mike, Mark and Terry were having their own problems. As Terry noted in a log he kept of my swim, *"Despite all our preparation, there was a lot of confusion. We were not prepared for the magnitude of what we were doing. It was very difficult to communicate in the dark when the grease board can't be read and stroke counts are taken by ear."*

Mike kept switching the spotlight on and off so, except for the constant orange glow of my lightstick, Terry's only knowledge of where I was and how fast I was swimming came from the unceasing sound of arm stroke after arm stroke entering the water. (These days with night swims, boat pilots are more apt to keep just their running lights on and put some well-placed light sticks along the side of the boat so they can see the swimmer and the swimmer isn't blinded.)

Terry proved to be a terrific crew member, and I greatly appreciated his efforts. He was in charge of timing and communication and performed his role superbly; the *Information Guru*. He took stroke counts, kept Mark informed of minute details, sighted for debris, recorded a log, and wrote messages to me on the grease board. He played lots of word games with me, naming state capitals and letting me know that certain people were thinking about me. Terry's written communications kept our talking at feedings to a minimum, thus saving precious time. His continual presence was reassuring.

5 AM: FIRST HOUR

By 5:30 a.m. the sky started to lighten just a bit and my anxiety lessened. I continued to feel strong, and it was comforting to be able to see the outlines of everyone on the boat instead of just the glare of the blinding spotlight.

During this hour, I began to see and read the grease board messages Terry wrote. Barring a catastrophe, I knew I would make it because there was absolutely no way I was going to quit or give up now. As far as I was concerned, there was little novelty to this swim anymore. I was performing what I had been practicing for so long.

First Feeding

While Terry handled timing and communications, Mark took care of videotaping, photography, tracking the course with Mike, and feeding me. I received my first feeding after an hour and ten minutes of swimming.

One of Terry's major roles as part of the crew was timing, which included the time between feedings. Mike wanted the first feeding to come at one hour, no earlier. After that, they were planned for every half-hour but Terry pushed them to every 32 or 33 minutes which no one noticed so he kept it up. This scheduling eliminated a feeding by the end of the swim, thus saving time.

Chow Time!

I wish I had experimented more with feeding intervals. They seem to be different in cold as opposed to warm water. Since a swimmer is not sweating as much in cold water, fluid replacement is not as important but it is still critical. For a swimmer not acclimated to the cold, feedings may need to be administered more frequently than in warmer water for the warmth they provide. Because I was well acclimated to cold water, I needed the feedings more for nourishment than warmth. During my training, I should have tried 40 to 50 minute intervals between feedings for the first few hours, lessening the time intervals later in the swim as necessary. They were also too slow, lasting anywhere from 40 seconds to 1 minute 30 seconds. I might have improved my finishing time by several minutes with faster and less frequent feedings. In the English Channel, weather and tides don't wait.

I consumed various nutrients: a carbohydrate drink (sometimes by itself and sometimes mixed with protein powder and/or liquid Tylenol) bananas, Fig Newtons, animal crackers, and tea. I sucked on a lemon at most feedings to alleviate the swelling in my mouth caused by the salt water, and also took some Vaseline in my mouth to spread around with my tongue as I swam. Whatever hot liquids I did not feel like consuming, I dumped over my head. Anything for warmth!

I knew when a feeding was about to happen because I could see Mark getting everything ready. Mike would stop the boat as Mark extended the FDS pole to me. Treading water, I would grab the first cup filled with liquid, chug it, take the second cup of solids, tilt it towards my face and catch whatever I could in my mouth, chewing rapidly as I stretched my arms over my head, then across my chest, followed by clutching my knees to my chest to stretch my lower back. I would then grab the third cup which had Vaseline in it and, with my tongue spread it around my mouth as I started to swim again. If I was still chewing solids, I would roll over on my back and swim a few backstrokes as I either finished what was in my mouth or spit it out. Invariably, some of the Vaseline would be swallowed. Eating during a marathon swim is not an experience in fine dining.

Since this swim, I have continued to experiment and now realize that many of my feeding methods were inefficient in the Channel. Warm, energy-providing liquids, followed possibly

Terry Tyner, one of my superb, attentive crew members, "The Information Guru."

by some solid food, or energy gel, is the most *quickly consumed, effective food source for me. Mouthwash also livens up my mouth and alleviates the swelling, thus circumventing the lemons and Vaseline. Lastly, warm liquids no longer are dumped over my head since it can lead to a headache. They either get ingested or they go into the water.*

Mark noted on the videotape during this time that I was in a "good state of mind." He would only find out afterwards how I really felt during the beginning. At the time, my stroke rate was a quick 84 strokes per minute even though I fought the constant sideward chop coming from the east. Norman recorded in the official log that I was swimming at 2.2 miles per hour.

I had heard that currents at the end of the swim make the finish very difficult so I wanted to save strength for the end. The Calculation Queen just wouldn't quit.

6 AM: SECOND HOUR

The South Goodwin Lightship was now visible to the far east and the Varne Indicator Buoy could be seen on the western horizon. We were 3.8 miles from the English Coast.

Around two hours into it, I started to ease up my pace just a little. It was impossible for me to hide anything from my crew; Mike noticed my deceleration right away and reported it to Mark.

Within the next half-hour my stroke rate slowed to 72 strokes per minute as I rode the chop and felt a few waves break over me. Mark recorded, *"The boat is really rocking, but Marcia has a tougher swim out there."*

The boat was constantly rocked by the swells. Many of the swells in the English Channel are created by boat wakes that often travel up to ten miles before subsiding, unless they hit something such as a ship or small boat to slow them down. During my swim about 60 boats and ships passed in every direction, including several passes by the Hovercraft ferry. I was unaffected by any of the generated swells and fortunately no one crewing on the *Aegean Blue* got seasick. The English Channel is not for those with weak constitutions. At two hours 15 minutes into the swim a big P&O ferry bound for Dover passed by on the west sending the usual four to five foot wake towards us. When the wake hit the boat the chair Terry was sitting in was knocked over sending him flying backwards onto the deck. I thought it was hilarious; Terry was not amused.

The wind had dropped from Force 3 to Force 2 and the wave heights subsided to a more manageable one to two feet. [Wind is measured on a Beaufort scale, with ratings between Force 0 (totally calm) to Force 12 (hurricane force.)] The skies were gray and overcast. Terry noticed a lot of seaweed (flotsam) and trash (jetsam) in the water; cups, bags, and other debris that had been thrown from ships. My stroke rate remained steady at 72.

One of the many Channel ferries that passed me during my swim. (A bbbbbig bbbbboat!) I later found out this was the M.V. *Pride of Dover*, captained by Allen Ewart-James on that day.

As I swam further from shore, I could finally peek back and see the White Cliffs of Dover With the daylight increasing, I would glance back when I breathed, a waste of time and another thing that did not go unnoticed by my crew. Mark caught one of these peeks on videotape, narrating, *"Marcia is looking back at the White Cliffs, a big 'no no' that she'll appreciate later."*

Something else was slowing me down: watching the shipping traffic. It is quite something to see these gigantic ships pass as you swim, dwarfing the ferries. The closest I got to one of them was about 150 yards. I was an admitted tourist in the beginning but there was a lot to watch. By the half-way point, distance-wise, Terry had written on the grease board a few times, *"Stop looking around, you tourist!"* I finally did.

Mike also noticed that I kept attempting to pull down my silicone bathing cap and told me to stop it. Basically, I was looking for a diversion and an excuse if my attempt failed. Mike, through experience, sensed this. Although my cap did ride up a little because of rough waves, it stayed basically in place throughout the swim. Once I became comfortable in the water I stopped fidgeting with it. By that time I was trying to unpin my lightstick at feedings thinking it might be slowing me down, which it didn't. (I'm glad I still have it today as a souvenir.) If I had simply stopped fussing with myself, I might have gotten across the Channel a little faster.

AROUND 7AM: THE THIRD HOUR

I could actually see France about three hours into my swim but I didn't mention it and I didn't look again for a long time. Instead, I watched the action on the boat whenever I took a breath in that direction. To me, that 33-foot boat was a lifeline. From my distance of ten yards, it was comforting to see Mike, Mark, Terry, Norman, and Lance choreographing my crossing. I had heard of some (former) boat pilots who would watch television during a swim. I knew that everyone on our boat was completely committed to the success of my swim. Mike's expertise as a pilot and his extensive experiences with Channel swims, had a great deal to do with my success. He was aware of my pace the whole way, as indicated by my stroke rate and the distance covered every half-hour. When my stroke rate fell from the 84 to 72 early on, he indicated that to Mark.

Suddenly I wondered what was going on. Mark and Mike were conferring intensely in the wheelhouse. They were already very concerned with my pace, even though I had been swimming for only 3 hours. At the next feeding, Mark solemnly told me that because of my stroke rate of 72, "You're on pace for an 11 to 11 1/2 hour swim. Do you want to pick it up? If so, I have two ideas. You can either make up the time all at once close to France or you can do all-out sprints for 15 minutes of every hour, as you did in Maine. This should help you catch a tide which should push you towards Cap Gris Nez." I chose the 15 minute sprints.

These 15-minute Pick Ups gave me a renewed sense of speed. Just as in Maine, I dreaded seeing the 'sprint' sign but this was the real thing. I had to sprint now to make the tide. All the practice and good help in the world wouldn't mean a thing if I didn't perform now.

8 AM: THE FOURTH HOUR

Spirits in the Channel

Somewhere out in the middle of the English Channel, before I could distinctly see France and while my swim was still simply laborious, I said a few silent prayers to the overcast skies. *"Thank you, God for giving me the strength and ability to do this. Please show me that you are with me."*

Right then, a ray of sunlight beamed through a small opening in the clouds and hit me. Then it immediately became completely cloudy again. I knew I was not out there alone seeking my goal but I also realized I was working for it.

Many times during my swim I thought, "This is really cool. I'm actually swimming the English Channel." I was thankful for and conscious about having the ability to be where I was, to have these favorable conditions, and to have such a great crew.

Norman Trusty fit his job description as the official Observer. He kept his eyes on me the whole time except to note almost all of the 60 ships and boats that passed us. This is done in case verification of a swim is necessary through shipping logs. It would verify that a swimmer was in a certain place in the Channel at a particular time.

Fish-Eye View of the Boat

There is not a lot of scenery to watch as you swim the English Channel, so I wound up observing my crew on the boat. I could tell that for much of the trip Mike was navigating and mapping the course while Lance steered the boat. Mike also talked on the radio frequently to the ship pilots in the area, alerting them that there was a swimmer in the water and asking for the right of way. Boats and ships have the right of way over swimmers and a few swims have ended because a ship pilot would not yield. If Mark was faced with the choice of his wife being run over by a super tanker or being pulled from the water, I was fairly confident Mark would select the latter.

One of the things I didn't see was Mark and Terry eating, as they were considerate not to eat in front of me as I swam. Many of the sandwiches, drinks, and snack foods they had packed went uneaten since they were constantly in motion as crew members. Anyway, the boat's constant rocking seemed to suppress their appetites.

Jellies

I had two encounters with marine life in the English Channel. The first was with jellyfish. Call me paranoid but

I was constantly on the alert for them. Swimming in the dark totally freaked me out because I was completely blind to the water in front of me. Once it became light I had a little control over the situation; at least I could see where I was swimming. As we got away from the chalky English coast the water became amazingly clear and I could see far down into it. Even though there was little to see except descending darkness, I did spot lots of "jellies." Most of these dinner plate-sized blobs hovered safely five to ten feet below the surface, but a few did go right by me at shoulder level. Fortunately, I was spared.

Seaweed

I encountered two patches of seaweed, each a few hundred yards across, making me thankful for all those "head up" drills I had practiced. The first patch came during the fourth hour when I was out in the middle of nowhere, the second occurred near the coast of France. During this fourth hour encounter, for some unknown reason, I thought of my young niece and nephew singing their "ABCs." Hearing their tiny voices inside my head helped lessen the drudgery of this 300 yard seaweed swim. Struggling through dense seaweed is like going through the rubber skirt section of a drive-through car wash. It doesn't hurt but it feels a little too snug for comfort. Mark told me later that Mike had steered me around several larger patches. I had heard before my swim that jellyfish sometimes hang around seaweed. Ugh!

Mental Blahs, Then Machine-Like

Many swimmers experience a "down period" during their Channel swims. Often, swimmers experience these depressing moments after six hours. You're tired and cranky and the end is nowhere in sight, literally or figuratively. The only thing to do is to keep swimming and get through it. I experienced a "down period" very early on, between hours two to four. After this period I spent the next two hours (four through six) feeling great in every way, a well-paced machine forging through the waters of the English Channel, getting the job done. I plowed through the westbound shipping lanes and was into the eastbound lanes, having covered well over half the distance by this time. I was in a positive frame of mind, making my mission happen.

9 AM: THE FIFTH HOUR

Five hours and 19 minutes into the swim, Terry wrote on the grease board: "We can't see England anymore." This mentally blew me away for a moment. To think I could have swum far enough to lose sight of the land we had started from was mind boggling.

One of the many things Mark and Terry did to amuse me was to wear T-shirts that said "Cleveland's English

Channel Crew 1994." They started out wearing white T-shirts. About a third of the way over, they surprised me by changing into red T-shirts. For the last part of the swim, they wore a blue version. It was fun to watch this surprise fashion show—anything for amusement! Mark's blue shirt still bears the grease stains that he received when he hugged me after the swim.

It may seem odd that during such a monumental swim, having all these enormous physical and mental stresses converge upon me, I enjoyed being amused by my crew. Such entertaining levity distracted me from the on-going task. What I was doing, swimming for hours on end, does become automatic after a while. My fast rhythm was comfortable so I looked around for other entertainment. It is rather like juggling on a tight rope without a safety net and looking around to see if there is yet another ball to add.

At one point during this hour, I could see that Mark had submerged his hand in a bucket of water. I yelled, "What's wrong?"

Mark waved me off and told me that everything was "just fine."

I found out afterwards that as Mark was pouring some very hot water into a cup for one of my feedings, he scalded his hand but managed not to drop the cup! Mike provided the first aid by getting a bucket of cold Channel water and had Mark immerse his hand in it. (This was the same water I had been comfortably swimming in for the past several hours!)

10 AM: THE SIXTH HOUR

Still Cranking

Almost six hours into the swim, Mark was videotaping and narrated: *"We're well past half-way now, into the eastbound shipping lanes where there are fewer boats than in the westbound lanes. Marcia is in a really positive frame of mind. The Cliffs of France are well within sight."*

Mike and Mark were still very concerned about time (all Terry wanted was completion), and I was handling the hourly 15-minute sprints well. Because of them, I had reached the half-way point (distance-wise) close to the target Mike wanted if I was going to land on Cap Gris Nez. Mike had calculated my finish to be on Cap Gris Nez but this could change for any number of reasons. My stroke rate had increased to 80 strokes per minute and the water had calmed down a little, just as Nora had said it would, but swells continued to hit both the boat and me constantly. This was all part of the "fun."

Peeking at France

I looked towards the distant coast again to see if I could see France and now I could. The French coast at Cap Gris Nez is much more gently sloping than I anticipated and not nearly as imposing as the White Cliffs in England. I had expected a view similar to Omaha Beach in Normandy but Cap Gris Nez only rises about 100 feet above sea level. I also expected that the Lighthouse would be huge. It isn't;

it remains a simple coastal icon. During a feeding this hour, I finally said to my crew, "So I suppose that's France," indicating the mass of land we were approaching. Terry replied, "We were waiting for you to tell us that."

Cap Gris Nez, France and the Lighthouse.

I had heard that from water level, both coasts looked closer than they actually were so it would be a waste of time and energy to keep checking my progress every few strokes. Only during the last hour or so of the swim did I permit myself to sight the shore every 100 strokes. I forced myself to concentrate on counting strokes, but also gave myself a little reward as I counted off small bits of notable progress.

At one point, after making seemingly no headway for quite some time, I imagined there were two gigantic tug boats hooked up to the continent, one on southern Spain and one on southern France, and they were pulling the land away from me. It just never seemed to get any closer.

As we had planned before the swim, I received one Motrin tablet at my six hour feeding, following the one I had taken with breakfast hours before. This helped to alleviate the escalating pain in my shoulder—Mark had no idea how much I wanted this!

Pacers

Pacers are allowed to accompany a Channel swimmer, entering the water from the escort boat, no sooner than two hours after the start and swimming for no longer than one hour at a time with the swimmer before they must return to the escort boat. After an hour break, a pacer (the same or another) may enter the water again for the maximum of one hour, with the swimmer's and boat pilot's permission, of course. Pacers are allowed to aid the swimmer only by swimming alongside for company and/or to help maintain or pick up the swimmer's pace. They are not allowed to make physical contact with the swimmer in any way, but they are allowed to wear wetsuits, fins, two or more caps, etc: all those heat-retaining devices that are strictly banned for the Channel-crossing swimmer.

It is a personal decision to have a pacer, but swimmers are best advised to inform their crew ahead of time if they want someone to swim into shore with them. I thought I would need or want a pacer during my swim because in my long pool swims, the companionship cheered me up. Not so in the Channel. I got into my own rhythm and soon realized that it would be difficult for me to adapt to another person in the water. Also, my crew was doing a great job with entertainment so companionship was not necessary. Neither Mark nor Terry were exactly in a position to pace me either. However, after pacing Nora several times the following week during her magnificent Two Way, I would suggest having a pacer for multiple crossings. (Getting into and out of the rough, cold water several times during Nora's Two Way was extremely difficult and tiring for me but it was dwarfed by Nora's effort.)

11 AM: THE SEVENTH HOUR

Mike Oram was in frequent radio contact with the French Coast Guard which monitors all swimmers and their boats as they approach the French coast. They want to ensure that a swimmer does not use a swim as a means to immigrate into France and they also want to prevent British boats from fishing in French waters. They have the right to stop any boat and check passports. The French Coast Guard radioed "Good Luck" to me!

A pain in my left shoulder became apparent about 6 hours into the swim, and was getting progressively worse. I told Mark about it during the seventh hour, but knew there was nothing he could do for me. My stroke felt unbalanced as my right arm entered the water smoothly, followed by my slightly inefficient left arm. I was tiring but the faster

I swam, the sooner my shoulder would stop feeling these knife-like pains. Mike encouraged me by saying at one point, "It's only pain."

When Terry told me to sprint during this hour, I picked up the pace and kept it up until I reached France. My closing sprint had begun. I was getting impatient and I wanted to finish.

Long before I swam the Channel, I was concerned about what to think about during the swim since it had been described to me as "long, cold, and boring." (It's anything but.) I started to collect and write inspiring phrases on index cards, implanting hundreds of these phrases into my head. During the Channel swim Terry wrote these phrases, or his variations, on the grease board. I definitely had favorites. One phrase that started out as, "Only amateurs wear wet suits" turned into, "Real swimmers swim naked."

The phrase most clearly defining my mindset during my swim was **"YES YOU CAN!"** and I said it over and over again.

NOON: THE EIGHTH HOUR

From the boat, Mike would often give me the signal to kick more, something I had gotten lazy about. I thought Mike would be more of a task master, more draconian during my swim. Being prepared was key. Terry found that I would work for Mike in a way I didn't work for Mark or for him. I found Mike supportive but tough and extremely observant. I could not get away with anything.

At eight hours, we were still three miles from the French coast and we all just wanted to get there. Because of the hourly 15-minute sprints, the concern with time had eased somewhat but it was not gone. As I neared the European mainland the sun started to come out.

Around this time Mike held a carrot out on a pole to motivate me. I chased it for awhile which elevated my stroke rate from 80 to 84 strokes per minute. At the next feeding break Mike asked me: "You want a bite of my carrot?"

At this feeding the water was clear and my underwater stretching was quite visible. I asked Mark: "How am I doing?"

Of course, everyone was listening so I received a chorus of replies. With Mark's answer, I knew my husband understood one thing fundamentally important to me: "You're doing OK but you could be doing better."

I uttered an exasperated, "Thanks," but knew he was right. I had not yet achieved my goal of swimming from England to France. The job still needed to be finished. There would be no rest until I arrived in France.

Mike teased: "You're not doing too badly. We have less than three miles to swim and at the rate you're going it should take about four hours."

Fortunately I understood he was joking and, with a smile, replied: "You're swimming back, hon."

With my lucid response, Mike felt fairly confident at this point that I would make it but it had taken more than eight hours of constant determination. No one is guaranteed success in the English Channel.

One Brain Cell for Guidance

After eight hours of watching me swim the English Channel for the first time, the crew's conversation turned to multiple crossings. Terry remarked: "I find it difficult but not impossible to understand how someone would want to do this once. I find it impossible to understand why somebody wants to do this more than once."

Mike Oram couldn't resist. "After you've had the first operation it doesn't matter."

Terry wondered where this conversation was going.

Mike continued: "They (Channel Swimmers) have all their brain cells taken out and one put back for guidance. It's an advanced warning system following up on GPS (Global Positioning System). The next best thing to the US Dolphins: Channel Swimmers. One brain cell for guidance."

Mark and Terry just laughed and laughed.

Fortunately Mark caught this conversation on videotape. Mike appears to be giving some sort of promotional plug in the foreground as I swim along in the background, oblivious to the conversation.

The water was a beautiful clear sea green color. It was too deep to see through the 100 to 200 feet to the bottom but I was able to peer several feet down into the darkness, past the jellyfish, and over at the bottom of the *Aegean*

Blue. The water had been murky along the English coast and in Dover Harbour because of the chalk sediment from the White Cliffs, but the French coastline was alive with the same phosphorescent clouds I had swum through at Rockaway Beach. As the sun came out and we closed in on the French shore, the water color changed from a dark sea green to a lighter emerald green. It was beautiful and tied my memories of training at Rockaway to this adventure.

When I was near the French shore I saw a couple of seagulls and mentally murmured, *"Bon Soir"* since it was the afternoon. (I was close to France, and they were undoubtedly French seagulls.) I was in my element and loving it!

Contemplations

As we approached land, I thought about the D-Day invasion which had occurred 50 years before. The Allied troops encountered extremely rough weather and were following orders that risked their lives. I was here on a voluntary basis and whether or not I succeeded, I was never in any danger. It was a privilege to be in this position.

During these final hours, I thought about swimmers who develop problems late in their swims, such as hypothermia, nausea, disorientation and fatigue. I had forewarned my crew that it might get tough after six hours because I would have been in the water long enough to have all these problems set in. Mark and Terry knew that if these problems developed, the best thing to do was to simply keep moving forward for as long as was safely possible. The Channel can be a cruel place, a dasher of dreams for those who are unprepared for the worst, and even for those who are. Fairness is not her concern. My training was paying off, the weather was cooperating, and I cranked onwards.

Eight hours and 19 minutes into the swim, my stroke rate dipped to 72 strokes per minute for about 15 minutes. Even though I felt as if I was sprinting my heart out, I was tiring a bit and kicking more now, trying to bring it home as fast as possible. I wanted to get there.

The French Coast Guard had been audible on the boat's radio for quite some time and Cap Gris Nez was visible to the west. Mark narrated the video: *"The water is calmer than the first half. There aren't as many boats now. We'll swim into shore and the tide will push us across to the Cape (Cap Gris Nez.)"*

Just as Mike Oram had planned.

Twenty minutes later, at 8 hours, 39 minutes, we were 1.5 miles from Cap Gris Nez. Mark comments on the videotape: *"This is the tough part of the swim."*

The land didn't seem to get any closer and there were still a lot of things that might go wrong before I got to France. I just had to keep swimming.

My stroke rate had crept back up to 76 strokes per minute, but the swells, chop, and wind had also increased, just as Nora predicted. I could feel my right arm entering the water smoothly, still pulling through efficiently, but the left arm lacked efficiency. As much as I was trying to stretch out, to lengthen my stroke, and to mentally block out the pain, my left shoulder really hurt.

At 8 hours, 45 minutes, Terry wrote on the grease board, "1 1/2 miles to go, Becky's by your side."

This message delighted me and I could visualize Becky swimming right next to me, as she had all those training days at the Vanderbilt YMCA. With machine-like resolve, I increased my rate to 80 strokes per minute, and powered myself towards the French shore.

1 PM: THE NINTH HOUR

Terry watched me intently during the last hour as I fought the constant chop and waves. His presence was comforting and he knew I didn't like to be left alone. During this period Terry was only concerned about giving me information on how far I still had to swim and how fast I was closing.

Norman was waving me on from his bow seat. I wanted to scream, "I'm working as hard as I can!" but I remained silent and kept swimming. He was only trying to help since he knew what an accomplishment it would be to break ten hours. Everyone shared this sense of urgency.

My arms continued to slice through the beautiful clear water at the rapid rate of 80 strokes per minute.

At 9 hours, 14 minutes, Mark could see the strong, swift, choppy cross-currents and noted on the videotape: *"Marcia is working very hard. I'm very proud of her."*

Towards the end I was being pushed by one of the strongest currents I had ever encountered. When I could first see the lighthouse on Cap Gris Nez it was to my right. A short while later I caught sight of it straight ahead. Moments later I could see it on my left. Throughout the swim the current had rarely been in my favor but at this point it whipped around the Cape unpredictably. The hardest part of most England to France Channel swims comes at the end. Fortunately a rip tide pulled me in over the last half mile but I had to expend enormous effort to get to that point.

Cap Gris Nez does not post any "No Swimming" signs. No one in his or her right mind would swim there. The rough boulders and rocks make accessing the water difficult from the land and dozens of slippery drop-offs lead right into treacherous currents. There generally are no spectators on these rough, slick boulders, just occasional French fishermen at low tide.

Nine hours, 28 minutes into the swim, Mark noted: *"Marcia just refused her feeding. She wants to close on the swim."* I was completely focused on finishing. Food could wait.

The water was very choppy with "white horses" (a.k.a. "white caps") kicking up and I increased my stroke rate to 84 strokes per minute despite intense shoulder pain.

Some discussion of an escort to land with me developed between Mike and Mark during this time. Mike thought it might be a good idea for me to be accompanied to the rocks since the coast where I would land was extremely rough. Mark told Mike that I wanted to do it myself. Mike said: "We'll just tell her to be careful."

In the next 5 minutes the same rough conditions in which I had started my swim returned. There were two- and three-foot waves and it became very windy. I was getting hit in the face by westbound waves whenever I breathed to my left. But at least in the daylight I could see where I was going. All the training, all the everything, was paying off. Mark commented on videotape: *"Need I say more?"*

For the past two hours I had thought about pausing briefly to stretch out my left shoulder but had decided not to. By ignoring the pain I hoped that it would go away. At 9 hours, 30 minutes, I finally did take this long-contemplated ten-second stretch which somewhat alleviated the discomfort. This pain would linger for the next four months. I still feel it at times today, years later.

One of Terry's last messages read, "Less than 500 yards to go."

Because westward currents were pushing me, when I saw Terry's sign, I mentally calculated that I would be swimming for about another 750 yards, taking about ten minutes.

Three minutes later Mike instructed Mark and Terry to get the "Post Swim" bags ready. They contained old warm clothes, thermal blankets, a ski hat, and towels to wipe off some of the grease. Mike was concerned with getting me wrapped up afterwards. Mark told him I did not want my bathing suit cut off. (I knew someone who had this done in order to get them out of their suit quickly.) Mike replied: "As long as she doesn't ask for a warm shower it doesn't matter what she does."

Mark and Terry were also scrambling to record the finish with both a camera and the on-going videotape. They checked to make sure they would not run out of film at a critical moment.

I tried to stretch out my stroke and turn my arms over faster. I tried not to think about how much my left shoulder hurt. I summoned up a second wind and yelled to myself, "Kick! Stretch it out! Turn it over! Dig down deep!" Big boulders were directly in front of me and I knew I was going to land on one of them.

Terry wanted to know how close the boat was going to get to shore. Lance answered with great precision: "Pretty close."

Since I was in good shape I would swim to the rocks by myself, as planned, leaving the boat in deeper water, about 75 yards from shore. If I had any problems, the *Aegean Blue* had a dinghy which could have escorted me to shore.

The last grease board message I received read, "9 HOURS 40 MINUTES, CAREFUL LANDING."

My boat crew let me make a judgment about the time. I was ecstatic! Nora had done a 9:40 on June 30th and I was so incredibly happy to be in the same ballpark as her. I left my shoulder pain and boat behind in the deeper water and sprinted through the chop towards shore.

For the past half-hour, the water had gotten progressively lighter in color as it became shallower, but not until within yards of the shoreline could I actually see the rocky bottom. I had been swimming so hard that I seldom paid any attention to what was under me; instead I was focusing on what was in front of me. Seeing gigantic boulders under me now was wonderful!

At last my left hand hit a submerged boulder. I thought, "Oh my God, I made it," but I knew the rules stated I had to get to where there was no water in front of me. Everyone on the boat knew this too. I clawed my way onto the barnacle-covered boulders.

Standing Victorious on the Rocky French Shore.
(I'm the one in the circle.)

The water was rough and the air was windy. I tried to stand up but waves and strong currents knocked me over a few times. No matter what, my swim would not be officially over until I got to the point where there was "no water in front of me." As I crawled forward I sensed a big drop-off (we found out later it was seven feet!) so I held on tightly to a boulder and let the wave subside before making another attempt towards the drier land ahead. I lunged to the next boulder, crawled a few more feet forward, and managed to stand up. There was no water in front of me. The boat horn sounded, signaling my finish. I had made it! I had just swum the English Channel on July 29th, 1994, in exactly 9 hours, 43 minutes, 31 seconds. I had accomplished my goal.

I was breathing hard and bent over to catch my breath, resting my hands on my thighs. (This time it was OK to get grease on them.) I waved to my crew, completely thankful for their assistance. I could hear everyone yelling from the boat and was grateful for their help to make my dream a reality. The elation and relief were enormous. I could finally stop working as hard as I had been working. It had been a long, long time in the making and everything had actually worked out. Here I was—finally—on Cap Gris Nez, France.

The finish had been both intense and paradoxical. I could not wait to stop swimming, yet I wanted this feeling of accomplishment to last forever. I was so incredibly happy and I wanted to savor this moment, to have it last and last. It was a satisfying feeling to have swum the English Channel.

I climbed up on top of a big boulder and sat down. Mike teased me later, "You Americans always have to sit on the biggest rocks!"

I watched the waves crash onto the rocks in front of me. From my perch I took in the glorious scene, alternating looking out on the Channel and up at the Lighthouse, thinking, "Wow! I did it! That was incredible!"

I wanted Mark to be with me now on that rock even though I could see him waving from the boat. He had been such an enormous part of my success and also deserved this amazing view.

Beyond the *Aegean Blue*, I could see lots of boats and ships rocking in the swells of the English Channel and I thought, "I just *swam* through *that*. It was *incredible* that I could get my body to do that. I can't even see the other side. Wow!"

I was awestruck and overwhelmed as I realized the magnitude of my feat. It is still sinking in years later.

On the boat, Mark reported on videotape: *"The English Channel has just been swum."*

Incredulously Terry remarked, "She just swam the English Channel."

They both played enormous roles in my swim, and seeing it culminate was amazing for all of us.

2 PM: BACK TO THE BOAT

Slowly, finally, three and a half minutes later, I climbed down off the rocks and swam the 100 yards back to the boat. I was tossed around a lot in the turbulence which was fine. The sense of tense urgency was gone. What a relief!! What joy!!

I bobbed in the clear waves and rocked in the swells before reaching the boat. I rolled over on my back, took a couple of strokes, rolled onto my stomach and swam a little breaststroke. I felt so relieved. Mark applauded as I grinned and shouted, "Thanks!"

He wanted to know if the swim had been boring. With the breath of someone who has been in constant motion for the past 9 hours and 44 minutes, I told him, "No, it was just so rough. Those last 2 1/2 hours were really, really hard and that finish was incredible. It was very tough."

As I touched the ladder, Mark said, "You did a 9:44." I smiled; I was very happy.

Mark hugged and kissed me when I got to the top of the ladder. I thanked him and cried out with conviction, "I _**did**_ it!"

We were both elated. He had been such an important part of this swim and it felt great to be together again.

Mike was impressed with my conditioning and my acclimation. To be able to sustain the pace I did for the last three hours and then not show any signs of being cold afterwards indicated exceptional training and preparation.

Terry took my bathing cap and goggles from me as Mark put a ski hat on me and unpinned my lightstick. He handed me a towel which I used to wipe off the little bit of grease that remained on my body, and then I donated

Savoring the Moment with Mark afterwards.

the towel to Mike's ever-growing collection. With some assistance, I managed to dress in an old, long-sleeved T-shirt and a sweatshirt, an old pair of sweat pants, heavy socks, and moccasins. Over this outfit went a thermal blanket and one of Mike's wool blankets. With Mark's arms wrapped around me, I was warm and happy.

We set off well but soon another returning Channel boat signaled for help. A relay team from London that had started an hour before me had just finished west of Cap Gris Nez. The boat's pilot indicated that one of his propellers had become disabled and asked if we would be willing to accompany them back to the Western Docks at half speed. The rules of the sea stipulate that one boat never leaves another one disabled, so, of course, we were willing. I was fairly oblivious to this quick agreement: a haze of elated exhaustion had set in. Instead of the usually

3+ hour boat trip, it took about 4 1/2 hours to return to England.

I felt a little nauseous from all the swells. It was incredible to watch them and think, "Wow, I just swam through all that rough water." I wanted to sit down in order to stabilize my motion and combat fatigue which was setting in rapidly. I was also extremely thirsty so Terry kept giving me bottled water. Although I was not particularly hungry, a sweet raisin scone found its way into my stomach. An hour later, because I was drinking so much, I needed to use the head. Even though I was only below deck for a very brief time, thanks to all the rocking and boat fumes, that raisin scone quickly found its way out of my stomach and over the side when I emerged from below. Then I felt much better.

Back at the Victoria Guest House, Bill and Audrey Hamblin had called the *Aegean Blue* several times during my swim to find out how things were going. Terry would convey their good wishes to me on the grease board, always making me smile. Twenty minutes after my finish I heard Mike talking to Bill and my mother on the boat's phone relaying the good news. Everyone was thrilled and Mom quickly began calling family and friends in the United States. After she spoke with immediate family members, Mom called my office which rapidly helped to spread the news. By the time *Aegean Blue* returned to England my assistant at work had called more than 100 people.

I was sort of drifting in and out of consciousness as I sat in a chair on the starboard side, wrapped in blankets, facing towards the west. Sometimes Mark was holding me and at other times he was part of the boat's activity. I cried quiet tears of joy and relief. It was starting to hit me that the reason I had been successful was because of all the hard work I had done. It was all worth it and came together in the final 2 1/2 hours of my swim.

For the last hour or so of the trip back to England, Mark, Terry, and I sat at the bow of the boat feeling like heroes as we motored into Dover. The wind had picked up in the late afternoon creating swirling streaks of clouds against the blue sky. I was feeling much less tired now than I had a few hours earlier. Most importantly, those silent questions that we all had at 3AM were answered: *Yes, she could! Yes, she did!*

As we pulled into the Western Docks, Mom and her friends greeted us with American flags and loud cheers. They were elated and relieved that everything had worked out. It was a very touching moment for all of us.

The celebration continued when we returned to Victoria Guest House. Audrey and Bill were thrilled; Nora was ecstatic, especially when I told her how much I had thought about her. Bill told me (jokingly) if I had not made it, "Your bill gets tripled and we leave your bags out on the street." They also thanked me for keeping their record intact!

My mother had joined us at the Guest House and helped me clean up in the upstairs bathroom. With disposable sponges and dishwashing detergent, she wiped off the grease that remained on my body. The grease around the nape of my neck just wouldn't come off in the tub so for a few days it was a constant reminder of my adventure, as if I needed one.

By the time I was dry and dressed, Mom, Mark and Terry had decided that we were going to *Topo Gigios*, an informal Italian restaurant in Market Square. I was OK with whatever decisions were being made for me now. My "Post Channel" life had just begun and I hadn't thought too much about it. No more schedules to follow for a while. I was simply enjoying myself.

Our dinner was jovial but calm since it had been a long day for all of us. Several other "Channel Wannabes" were there too, but few of them actually said anything to me.

With Mike Oram, on right, and Terry, on left, en route back to England, after a successful swim.

I noticed a sense of envious admiration. The thought, "I would love to be in your place now," came through loud and clear.

At our own table the togetherness was particularly nice at this special time. Everyone was just so happy and excited that my swim had worked out so well. How do you ever start explaining what happened?

I was not particularly tired or hungry at this dinner. In fact, on Friday and Saturday nights, I slept a normal eight hours, not the unusually long hours I had expected. However, for the next few days, I was extremely thirsty and my lips and mouth were parched from the sun and the salt water. For days I drank lots of water and applied Vaseline to my lips. Some great mouth lozenges we picked up at Boots helped ease my sore mouth. However, my left shoulder did have pain for the next four months. Fortunately the ache did not prevent me from smiling that "Channel smile" which made all the temporary aches and pains worthwhile. As Nora would say, "Vale la Pena!"

On Saturday morning Mark fulfilled his bet that if I swam the English Channel, he would swim in Dover Harbour for one second. He actually lasted 15 minutes in the 64°F water!

After a leisurely breakfast we went down to the Harbour and swam out to one of the boat moorings with Pierre Van Vooreen, the first Belgian to swim the English Channel. I was just so happy that I had done well. There were a number of people on the beach who had heard, and they congratulated me. Fred and Molly were delighted. I felt so relieved. I had crossed an enormous barrier in so many ways. I proved to myself that I could do it.

In the two days after my swim, Mark interviewed me on videotape. Phrases like, "It was really hard," and "It was an incredible experience," kept surfacing. The difference in my tension and confidence from two days earlier is quite noticeable.

We had a wonderful celebration dinner that Saturday night. Mom and her friends put this party together for Mark, Terry, and me, at the hotel where they were staying. The proprietor kept the champagne flowing all night and I just kept smiling and smiling. All evening I was in a delightfully pleasurable dream state.

I was incredibly happy.

Mark, Terry, and I stayed in Dover until Sunday July 31st, then set off to tour the southern English countryside and London for five days. Before my Channel crossing, I had enjoyed swimming in the Harbour. Old habits die hard and after my swim I continued swimming in the Harbour during our stay in Dover. But I distinctly remember feeling a sense of melancholy that my goal had been reached. I assured myself that these feelings were OK, and they are.

"Thumbs Up!" with Nora Toledano Cadena of Mexico in front of Victoria Guest House after my swim.

··

Crewing for Nora

Nora had asked me to be part of her crew and to pace her during her swim, and I gladly obliged. I kept in touch with Audrey while we were away from Dover to find out when Nora was going to swim. After eating dinner in London on Friday August 5th, Mark and I said goodbye to Terry who was flying back to New York the next day, then we drove back to Dover. Getting a room for Mark was weird, since it meant that I was spending my night on the boat.

We went over to Audrey and Bill's to meet Nora, then headed down to the Western Docks once again to load up the *Aegean Blue*.

As I had done on the previous Friday, Nora began her Channel swim from Abbot Cliff, England, at 11 p.m. on Friday August 5th.

At 10:38 p.m. on Saturday August 6th, 1994, after swimming for 23 hours and 38 minutes, Nora Toledano Cadena became the sixth women ever to swim a Two Way, a non-stop swim from England to France and back to England again. I was proud to be a part of her crew and her pacer for this incredible swim. She has written a book about her swimming experiences with her fellow Mexican natador, Antonio Argüelles.

I felt sad leaving Dover because of all the wonderful friends I had made there in such a short period, people with whom I shared a common passion. I correspond frequently with these friends from all over the world and even manage to see them occasionally. A 'Channel Swimmer' chat site now exists making it easy to stay connected with one another.

Life in and around the English Channel goes on.

Closing In On Cap Gris Nez Again

Two days after the completion of Nora's swim, on Monday August 8th, Mark and I took a ferry to Calais, France. From there, we visited Cap Gris Nez, approaching it by land this time. We crossed the Channel on one of the gigantic ferries we had just recently seen from a much different perspective. During the ride we stayed on the top open deck, just staring out at the water. I kept thinking and repeating, "Wow! I was actually down there stroking my way towards France!"

There is a small gift shop and restaurant at the base of the lighthouse at Cap Gris Nez and a few bed & breakfast inns within a half-mile of the Cape. I was surprised to find so much civilization there; I expected just a lighthouse and a couple of determined tourists.

We checked into one of the B & B's in the late afternoon and walked to the Cape as the sun was starting to set. The light was beautiful. There were several tourists around and I have to believe that many of them were thinking about the grand concept that "People actually swim from here to over there. It's so far away."

I was one of these Cap Gris Nez tourists now, but I had an entirely different feeling of intimacy with the Channel.

In the morning, Mark and I hiked down to the water, intent on finding the big boulder I had landed on. All our pictures had been developed in Dover so we were able to find the exact location. I felt it was important to check out the actual spot; doing this gives a sense of closure. *(Two years later, in 1996, when my first training partner, Robert Makatura, made his successful crossing, we again returned to Cap Gris Nez to find his landing spot. We have done the same each time I have been involved in a crossing.)*

Vacation!

Taking advantage of the fact that we were already abroad, Mark and I toured the Normandy Coast of France, visiting all of the D-Day beaches; stopped in on Pierre Van Vooren in Belgium one afternoon; and spent a few days exploring southwestern England. The entire trip was a joy as we basked in the elation and relief of my Channel swim.

We returned home to New York at midnight on Wednesday August 17th. My cousin had put a "Congratulations" banner in our apartment and several friends sent cards. I was really happy and knew that a new chapter of my life was about to begin, the previous one having been skillfully written.

TEN

Looking Back

IN ALL TIDAL WATER, TIDES SHIFT ABOUT every six hours and 10 minutes. In the English Channel this often results in a swimmer's course resembling a sine wave or an inverted letter 'S.' The faster you swim the less mileage you swim because you don't get pushed as far side to side by the tides. Swimmers who just miss Cap Gris Nez are usually pushed east by the high tide into Wissant Bay and sometimes further along to Calais, (20 kilometers/13 miles from Cap Gris Nez), hence the bottom tail of the 'S.' If a swimmer is pushed west from Cap Gris Nez by a low tide he or she may have to swim parallel to the rocky French coast for miles, unable to get to shore because of the strong currents.

My course wound up being about 30 miles long and resembled an inverted 'V' or the numeral '7,' which is close to the route that Mike Oram had in mind. I was lucky to hit Cap Gris Nez but I had had to work for it.

The first time I saw my course was when the *Aegean Blue* was pulling into the Western Docks after the 4 1/2 hour boat trip back across the Channel. Mike had charted our position on his map of the Channel as I swam. I was amazed. Except for the very end, I never realized I had been swimming any way but straight across. My angled course astounded me and I asked Mike about it.

"Oh, yes. This is where the high tide turned," he said, pointing to the exact vortex of my course on his map.

Mike went on: "I wanted you out a little further so you wouldn't have to work as hard as you did at the end. If you had been a mile or less further towards France when the tide turned, you would have had a straight line into Cap Gris Nez and wouldn't have had to sprint for three hours to hit the Cape."

All of these predictions came as a result of Mike's experience and careful pre-planning of my swim.

His analysis continued as he pointed to my course on the map. "Here's where you eased up after two hours (the half-hour marks are close together denoting less distance) and here's where you picked it up." (The marks are much further apart.)

It pays to swim fast in the beginning of a Channel crossing, but several unknown trade-offs exist such as the weather, the French currents, potential exhaustion and the cold water.

According to Mike Oram, we reached the halfway distance point at 4 hours and 52 minutes, meaning I "even split" my swim, time-wise. Looking at the course map, it shows I covered substantially more distance in the second half than in the first so I "negative split" my English Channel swim, distance-wise.

ELIMINATING THE FACTORS

Water Temperature and Acclimation

The water temperature was a factor I had eliminated over a period of two years. On July 28th, the day before my swim, the temperature was 14° Celsius (57.2° Fahrenheit) in the middle of the Channel and 15° Celsius (59° Fahrenheit) along the shore. Acclimating to cold water is not a process that can be rushed and hypothermia is a major cause of failure.

The only time I ever felt cold during my Channel swim was at the very beginning when my toes and shoulders felt chilled. I figured out later that I had crawled up the cold stone beach at the start which probably made my toes cold. When the grease mixture on my shoulders hit the cold water it chilled me a little. Aside from these episodes at the start, I was always comfortable with the water temperature. During my sixth hour feeding I even remarked to my crew, "This water temperature feels good!"

By the time I reached France at midday the sun had come out and I estimate that the water was about 62°F; a relative bathtub!

Head Thoughts

One of the most frequent questions I get asked about my Channel swim (and open water swimming in general) is "What do you think about when you swim?"

Like most open water swimmers, every song ever written has played in my head at one point or another. During my Channel crossing, the BC-52's version of *The Flintstones* theme song went through my head for a long time. It was popular on the radio during the summer of 1994 and it's quick, repetitive, and uncomplicated tune made it perfect for a long swim. I also sang my ABC's (the kiddy version), which I found helpful for putting together lots of sets of 30 strokes. At one point, the current British pop song *I Saw The Sign* piped in loud and clear. As I drew closer and closer to France my thinking narrowed to the single, determined, focused thought, "Get there!"

IMMEDIATE REFLECTIONS

Approaching France

In the "Post-Swim" video interview that Mark did during the two subsequent days following my Channel swim, I described the approach to France. "At the three hour feeding I could see France. It was this far-off mass of land. As I got closer, the mass turned into colors, then the colors eventually turned into objects. Soon I could see the lighthouse on Cap Gris Nez and I could see green grass and cliffs and then there were rocks at the base of the cliffs and suddenly I was climbing on the boulders. It was just an incredible experience."

It occurred to me during this interview that the fine scratches all over my palms and legs were from crawling over the barnacle-covered boulders at Cap Gris Nez. I was oblivious to the scratches when I received them and they never hurt. It was nice to think about where they came from every time I rubbed my scratched-up palms together.

LONGER TERM REFLECTIONS

My English Channel swim was different than I expected, not harder or easier, but different. I had trained in conditions that closely simulated those in the Channel. I expected the swim to be more melodramatic, more of a "life or death" situation. It turned out to be a calm and controlled swim because the weather was decent, I was prepared, and my boat pilot and crew were excellent.

Swimming the English Channel has helped me to understand that big things take time and occur as a result of a long-term process. The Channel also introduced me to a new and higher standard of challenge. It allows one the opportunity to explore his or her limits. You find out how far you can go and you discover that you can probably go even farther.

In the days after the event I thought about the training I had done and realized that I was not over-trained. Because of all the training I did, I was able to sustain the increased pace I held over the last one-third of the swim.

PERKS

What does one receive for swimming the English Channel? You get a complimentary photocopy of the official observer's log. You are also allowed to buy several apparel items: pins, bathing caps, and a beautifully inscribed vellum scroll with your name, swim time, and date, all signed by the officers of the swim organization with which you swam. You also get to tell everyone you want to for the rest of your life that you swam the English Channel. But more importantly, from an intrinsic perspective, I know I did it and I know what it took, and those two factors are a commanding way to summon inner strength. *"Wow, I did it!"* is a powerful internal phrase for me.

Channel Swimming Association

Comdr. C. Gerald Forsberg O.B.E., R.N.
President

This is to certify that

Marcia Cleveland

swam the English Channel

England to France

on 29th July 1994 in 9 hours 44 minutes.
Trainer ~ Mark Green   Crew ~ Terry Tyner
The swim was duly entered in the
Record Book of the Association
on 23rd September 1994

Gerald Forsberg President.

Michael P. Read Chairman.

Michael Oram Hon. Secretary.

EPILOGUE

I WILL ALWAYS REFLECT ON MY ENGLISH Channel swim with satisfaction and pride, knowing I did a good job. Now I am on to other goals and directions in life.

We all have chapters in our lives. While the first edition of this book was being written, Mark and I prepared for another remarkable chapter, "The Birth of Julia Cleveland Green on February 12, 1998." Julia was joined by her brother, Samuel Wherly Green, on December 28, 2000. Mark and I are now deep into the throes of parenthood with much of our current time and energies directed towards our children.

The Channel also changed the relationship between Mark and me, deepening our trust in each other and sharpening the communication between us. We did something in which we both played instrumental roles, sometimes under a lot of stress, and we were able to pare our thoughts down quickly to the core level and reap the benefits. As we face difficult life situations in which the only 'out' is through the rough seas of life, we are armed with the mental focus and physical stamina to dig down deep and persevere through these difficulties. Our marriage continues to grow all the time as we create more and more of a life together.

Together, Mark and I also gained a clear understanding of what is involved in a Channel swim: a Channel swim is best experienced by living it.

Most people directly involved with this adventure refer to it in a plural, possessive form, such as "our swim." This was rightfully the case for my swim since it was my boat pilot and crew that enabled me to be successful. When Mark interviewed me after crossing the Channel, without any conscious intention, I regularly referred to the swim in plural form, "*We* started picking it up which put *us* in decent position." "*We* wanted to make Cap Gris Nez otherwise *we* would have been in the water another two hours." Boat pilots and crew members are entitled to such possessive recognition since they are the ones who guide the swimmer.

When Mark and I returned from England in August my office colleagues threw a surprise party for me and invited many of my clients. They presented me with a beautiful Tiffany silver platter engraved with the English and French coasts and my name, swim time, and date. I was amazed, touched, and very grateful.

After living in Riverside, Connecticut for 8 years and swimming regularly in the Long Island Sound, our family moved to Winnetka, Illinois in July 2003, a suburb north of Chicago. I remain active in swimming today and continue to compete in open water and pool competitions. As a result of my swimming, Mark and I have friends all over the world and this wonderful, tight-knit community continues to grow.

Since my own Channel swim, I have advised numerous aspiring Channel swimmers towards successful swims and am glad to assist with others. Some of the most significant teachings I received from my Channel swim was the responsibility to help others and to give back to the sport. I have returned to Dover several times to assist fellow swimmers and to swim relays. Every time I am in the Channel I am awestruck at its size, beauty, and temperamental nature. To swim the Channel is always an extraordinary feat.

On August 1, 1996, I established a new women's American record around Manhattan Island, completing the 28 1/2 mile course in 5 hours, 57 minutes, 53 seconds. On August 2, 2005, I completed a solo crossing from Catalina Island to the California Mainland in 8 hours, 56 minutes, with two others swimmers, Liz Fry and David Blanke. There have been lots of other swims and there always will be!

Although my family is my top priority, swimming will always be a part of my life. Even with my super-busy schedule, I make sure swimming and fitness remain within the big picture. I now develop coached swim programs for swimmers of various ages and ability levels, conduct open water clinics, and give private instruction. You may reach me through SwimMarcia.com or DoverSolo.com.

I am involved in United States Masters Swimming in several areas, most obviously with the Long Distance Swimming Committee.

Every year, on July 29th, I celebrate my Channel Anniversary in some small, personal way.

Until the birth of our daughter, Julia, I worked in advertising sales and direct marketing. Being a constant and integral part of Julia and Sam's lives is gratifying to me. My days are full, challenging, and satisfying. The abundance of rogue waves and unpredictable winds and currents keep things interesting.

Every time I leave Dover, I don't wonder *if* I will return; I only wonder **when**.

Marcia, Mark, Julia, & Sam, December 2007.

APPENDIX

INSPIRATIONS

ACKNOWLEDGEMENTS

TEMPERATURE CONVERSION CHART

DISTANCE CONVERSION CHART

IMPORTANT ADDRESSES

SWIMMING CONTACTS

INSPIRATIONS

Some inspirational sayings from my note cards:

- SUCCESS IS A RESULT, NOT A GOAL.
- If we can dream it, we can do it.
- Obstacles are what we see when we take our eyes off the goal.
- There are no great people; rather, there are great challenges that ordinary people meet.
- It's almost over, I know I can finish. The difficult part is behind me.
- Unless I face the challenge and take the risk, I'll never know what I can do.
- I am willing to work as hard as I have to because I want to succeed.
- Ask not for victory alone, ask for courage. For if you can endure you bring honor to yourself. Even more, you bring honor to us all.
- Tough as Nails!
- YES, YOU CAN!

Inspirational Biblical Passages:

Romans 8:18

I consider that the sufferings of this present time are not worth comparing with the glory that is to be revealed to us.

Romans 5: 3-5

More than that, we rejoice in our sufferings, knowing that suffering produces endurance and endurance produces character, and character produces hope and hope does not disappoint us, because God's love has been poured into our hearts through the Holy Spirit which has been given to us.

Hebrews 12:11

For the moment all discipline seems painful rather than pleasant; later it yields the peaceful fruit of righteousness to those who have been trained by it.

Ideas and questions aspiring Channel swimmers may want to think about:

What is your goal?

Remember your goal. Stay focused on it.

Do you know what is involved?

Are you able to do the necessary training in light of your current family, work, and life situation? Do you have their support?

Take full responsibility for your training.

Set up the building blocks every day, every week, every month, to get you across the Channel.

Do you accept the work needed to swim the English Channel?

It's really hard: why do you think you can do it?

Are you self-reliant?

Have you made detailed notes of how you are going to tackle each factor?

Are you willing to do what it takes to have a good swim?

Accept the concept of being tired, of going to practice again and again even though you feel you're exhausted.

Your aim is a straight line and this is what you're training for and this is what makes the swim so challenging. You are tired and the currents are very strong. With the proper training, you have the ability to make it but you must apply yourself. Will you?

You most likely will experience training plateaus.

Be honest with yourself; this builds confidence.

You're out there in the middle of almost nowhere and the outcome is entirely up to you.

ACKNOWLEDGMENTS

I give my thanks and appreciation to my husband, Mark Green, whose love, support, and caring allowed us to cross the English Channel together.

I also want to thank Terry Tyner who was an outstanding crew member. And to Mike Oram, thank you for your experience and high expectations for all your swimmers.

I thank my parents, Carolyn Cleveland and Bob Cleveland for helping me in Maine, and Mark's parents, Yolanda and Philip Green, for the support they provided.

To Robert Makatura, Marcy MacDonald, and Becky Fenson, my training partners, thanks for all the fun times together and sharing the hard work. It was worth it for all of us. It's always a pleasure to swim with all of you!

To Nora Toledano Cadena, your reassuring advice was indispensable and your friendship, a dear one.

Thank you, Judy Lohman, for pushing me to write this book, and for assisting with the editing. I also give you full credit for coming up with (and insisting upon) the title, *Dover Solo*.

Many thanks to Yolanda Green, Jean Altman, and Morris Finkelstein who offered excellent editing ideas, and to Gwen Deely who lent a reliable flipper with the maps.

I appreciate the help of family and friends too numerous to name who supported all my Channel efforts. Thanks to the members of Red Tide Masters Swim Team, Team New York Aquatics, and all the encouraging people I swam with in New York City during my training.

And thanks to the 444 brave Channel swimmers who preceded me. Good luck to those who wish to follow!

TEMPERATURE CONVERSION CHART

CELSIUS	FAHRENHEIT	FAHRENHEIT	CELSIUS
9	48.2	48	8.9
10	50.0	50	10.0
11	51.8	52	11.1
12	53.6	54	12.2
13	55.4	56	13.3
14	57.2	58	14.4
15	59.0	60	15.6
16	60.8	62	16.7
17	62.6	64	17.8
18	64.4	66	18.9
19	66.2	68	20.0
20	68.0	70	21.1

Celsius to Fahrenheit = [(Degrees C. × 1.8) + 32]
Fahrenheit to Celsius = [(Degrees F. − 32)/ 1.8]

DISTANCE CONVERSION CHART

MILES	YARDS	METERS	KILOMETERS
1	1,760	1,610	1.61
2	3,520	3,220	3.22
3	5,280	4,830	4.83
4	7,040	6,440	6.44
5	8,800	8,050	8.05
6	10,560	9,660	9.66
7	12,320	11,270	11.27
8	14,080	12,880	12.88
9	15,840	14,490	14.49
10	17,600	16,100	16.10
11	19,360	17,710	17.71
12	21,120	19,320	19.32
13	22,880	20,930	20.93
14	24,640	22,540	22.54
15	26,400	24,150	24.15
20	35,200	32,200	32.20
25	44,000	40,250	40.25
30	52,800	48,300	48.30

35	61,600	56,350	56.35
40	70,400	64,400	64.40
45	79,200	72,450	72.45
50	88,000	80,500	80.50

1 Mile = 1,760 Yards   1 Kilometer = 1,000 meters

To convert Miles to Kilometers: # Kilometers × .621)

To convert Kilometers to Miles: (# Miles × 1.61)

IMPORTANT ADDRESSES

Mr. Mike Oram
Honorable Secretary
Channel Swimming & Piloting Federation
The Hermitage
12 Vale Square
Ramsgate, Kent CTI 19BX
England
Telephone from the United States: 011-44-(1) 843-852-858
Main Telephone: +44 (0)843 852858
E-mail: Michael.Oram@btinternet.com
Websites: ChannelSwimming.com, ChannelSwimming.net
Website for all Solo Channel Crossings: www.Channel-Swims.info

Audrey and Bill Hamblin
Victoria Guest House
1 Laureston Place
Dover, Kent CT16 1QX
England
Telephone from the United States: 011-44-1304-205-140

There are several other excellent Guest Houses in the Dover area which generously cater to Channel Swimmers and their families.

Dr. Julie Bradshaw
Honorable Secretary
Channel Swimming Association
381 New Ashby Road
Loughborough, Leics LE11 4ET
England
Telephone: +44 (0)1509 554137
E-mail: swimsecretary@ntlworld.com
Website: Channelswimmingassociation.com

SWIMMING CONTACTS IN THE UNITED STATES

United States Masters Swimming
P.O. Box 185
Londonderry, NH 03053-0185 USA
Telephone: 603-537-0203
Website: http://www.usms.org
Open Water Information: http://www.usms.org/longdist/
E-mail: usms@usms.org

USA Swimming
One Olympic Plaza
Colorado Springs, CO 80909-5770
Telephone: 719-578-4578
Website: http://www.usa-swimming.org

Mr. Randy Nutt
Aqua Moon Adventures
2615 NW 99 Avenue
Coral Springs, FL 33065 USA
Telephone: 954-821-3294
E-mail: info@randynutt.com
Web: www.AquaMoonAdventures.com

How to get in touch with me:
Marcia Cleveland
www.DoverSolo.com
www.SwimMarcia.com
E-mail: Doversolo@aol.com

Made in the USA